THE HEALTHY JUNIOR CHEF

COOKBOOK

PHOTOGRAPHY BY
ERIN SCOTT

weldon**owen**

Vanilla-Coconut Bundt Cake (page 116)

CONTENTS

Sweet Potato Tacos with Black Beans,
Corn & Avocado (page 116)

INTRODUCTION

Learning to cook is both fun and rewarding—especially when you share the healthy and delicious results with family and friends. In the following pages, you will find all you need to know to get started in the kitchen: an illustrated guide to basic techniques, a treasure trove of handy tips to streamline culinary tasks, and more than 65 easy-to-follow recipes, from simple breakfasts, hearty soups and salads, and satisfying mains to yummy snacks and mouthwatering desserts. Don't be put off by the word healthy. In this book, healthy equals tasty, so keep an open mind and you'll quickly discover wonderful new flavors in every dish.

In cooking as in all skills, practice makes perfect! Whenever you try a recipe for the first time, you are likely to learn something you didn't know about a technique, an ingredient, and/or your own personal taste and style. The recipes' step-by-step instructions and tips are there to help you succeed with that new knowledge. Grown-ups are great for sorting out any questions you may have as you cook. Make sure at least one adult is always nearby to help keep you safe when oven and stove-top heat, sharp knives or special tools, or fully loaded pots and pans are involved.

Whether you decide to make banana pancakes to power you up after a sleepover, chewy granola bars to snack on after school, or sweet potato tacos for the dinner table, this book will help you build your culinary confidence with a new and exciting repertoire of healthful favorites everyone will love. So roll up your sleeves, tie on an apron, and get ready to begin an adventure you will enjoy throughout your life.

HEALTHY TECHNIQUES

ORGANIZATION

Whether you want to make an afternoon snack for yourself or a full meal for your family, the first thing you must do is set up your *mise en place*, French for "everything in its place." Before you begin to cook, carefully read through the recipe from start to finish. Next, gather all the ingredients and equipment you'll need. Then, prepare the ingredients as much as possible and arrange them neatly around your work area for easy access. As you work, keep your hands and the surrounding surfaces clean. Promptly clear away whatever you have finished using, dropping dirty utensils into the sink and putting ingredients back into the cupboard or the fridge. A few blunders are bound to happen, but *mise en place* can help you prevent most kitchen errors.

BASIC TECHNIQUES

Knife Skills

Learning how to use a knife is an essential kitchen skill for two primary reasons: the safety of the cook and the preparation of many ingredients. When choosing which knife to use, first consider the item to be cut and then select a knife that is suitable to the task and feels comfortable in your hand.

To hold a kitchen knife properly, grasp it firmly by the handle, as if you were shaking someone's hand. Hold down the item you are cutting with your other hand, placing the food flat side down whenever you can and curling your fingers under your knuckles to keep your fingertips out of harm's way. With the tip of the knife pointing down, start to cut, bringing the handle straight up and down and always cutting away from your body. Follow the directions on the facing page for how to chop, slice, and dice most fruits and vegetables.

Measuring

Knowing how to measure with precision is key to success in the kitchen, especially when you're baking. For small amounts of liquid and dry ingredients, you will need a set of measuring spoons (usually ¼ teaspoon, ½ teaspoon, 1 teaspoon, and 1 tablespoon). For liquids, use clear measuring pitchers with a ruler printed vertically on the side and a lip for pouring, and for dry ingredients, such as sugar and flour, select flat-topped measuring cups. Follow the directions on the facing page for the correct measuring techniques.

HEALTHY CHOICES

Consuming foods you have cooked yourself is the first step in healthy eating. Many ultra-processed foods carry added sugars and sodium, unhealthy fats, additives, and more. The recipes in this book take a balanced approach to healthy eating, sticking to a few basic tenets of a good diet: a focus on vegetables and fruits, whole grains, low-calorie proteins, and reduced sugar and sodium and a thumbs-down to ultra-processed foods (always read a package label before you buy). Combine these smart food choices with a sport or other physical activity you like and you're well on your way to a healthy lifestyle. Don't forget to drink lots of water too! It will help keep you hydrated and energized and feeling good.

» HOW TO SLICE

1 Lay the item to be cut firmly on the cutting board, first trimming a thin slice from one side if needed to rest it flat.

2 Holding the item to be cut with curled fingers to keep fingertips safe, slice with the knife blade perpendicular to the cutting board.

3 Slice the food while resting the flat side of the knife blade gently against your knuckles, allowing them to guide the width of your slices.

» HOW TO CHOP

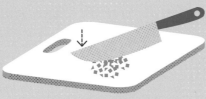
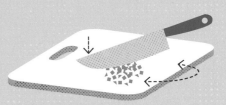

1 Grasping the handle of the knife with one hand, hold the tip of the knife against the board with the other hand.

2 Keeping the knife tip steady, raise the handle up and down in a chopping motion.

3 As you move the handle up and down, sweep the knife back and forth in a slow arc until the ingredient is chopped as desired.

» HOW TO DICE

1 Cut the item to be diced in half. Lay each half, cut side down, on the cuttting board.

2 Cut each half into even slices the same width as your intended dice, working lengthwise if the item is long.

3 Cut the long slices into lengthwise strips, then turn and cut crosswise into dice.

» HOW TO MEASURE

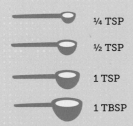

¼ TSP

½ TSP

1 TSP

1 TBSP

Check liquid measurements at eye level to ensure accuracy.

Spoon dry ingredients into a flat-topped measuring cup until mounded on top. Using the back of a knife, sweep off the excess level with the rim of the cup.

BREAKFAST

» OAT FLOUR lends texture and protein to these satisfying pancakes. If you can't find oat flour at the market, you can make it by finely grinding old-fashioned rolled oats in a food processor.

BANANA-OATMEAL PANCAKES

Serve the pancakes hot from the frying pan, or keep them warm in a 200°F oven while you cook the others. Bananas, raspberries, and pecans are a flavorful trio of toppings, but you can swap in any of your favorite berries or nuts, if you like.

1 MAKE THE BATTER

In a large bowl, whisk together the flours, baking powder, baking soda, cinnamon, and salt. Add the oats, maple syrup, egg, milk, vanilla, and coconut oil and mix with a rubber spatula just until combined. Be careful not to overmix.

2 COOK THE PANCAKES

Heat a large frying pan or stove-top griddle over medium-high heat. When the pan is hot, add 1½ teaspoons coconut oil, and when it melts, spread it evenly over the surface of the pan with a spatula. Using a large ice cream scoop, drop a scoopful of the batter into the hot pan for each pancake, spacing them about 2 inches apart. Reduce the heat to medium and place a few banana slices on top of each pancake. Cook until the edges start to firm up and turn golden and bubbles appear on the surface, 2–3 minutes. Using the spatula, flip the pancakes, reduce the heat to low, and cook until the second side is golden brown, 1–2 minutes longer. Be careful not to let the bananas burn, adding more coconut oil to the pan if they start to scorch before the pancake is cooked through. Using the spatula, transfer the pancakes to a plate and keep warm. Repeat with the remaining batter, adding more coconut oil to the pan as needed.

3 SERVE THE PANCAKES

Put the remaining bananas, raspberries, and pecans in separate serving bowls. Serve the pancakes piping hot with maple syrup, bananas, raspberries, and pecans for adding at the table.

1 cup oat flour

1 cup all-purpose flour

2 teaspoons baking powder

1 teaspoon baking soda

1 teaspoon ground cinnamon

1 teaspoon salt

1 cup old-fashioned rolled oats

¼ cup maple syrup, plus more for serving

1 large egg, lightly beaten

1½ cups whole milk

1 teaspoon pure vanilla extract

1 tablespoon coconut oil or unsalted butter, melted, plus more for cooking the pancakes

2 bananas, peeled and sliced

1 cup fresh raspberries

½ cup lightly toasted chopped pecans

FRUIT & COCONUT CHIA PUDDING OVERNIGHT JARS

Soaked in liquid such as the nut milk in this recipe, chia seeds soften and develop a gel-like texture and look similar to tiny tapioca balls. Packed with fiber, protein, and cold-fighting antioxidants, they were part of the daily diet of the Aztecs and Mayans, who consumed them to maintain their stamina.

1 MAKE THE PUDDING

Have ready 2 pint jars with lids. Add to each jar ¼ cup of the milk, 1 tablespoon of the chia seeds, 1½ teaspoons maple syrup, and 1 dash of vanilla and then stir well. Cover and refrigerate for at least 4 hours or up to overnight.

2 FINISH & SERVE THE PUDDING

Stir the chia mixture in each jar, then let the jar stand at room temperature until the seeds are plumped, about 10 minutes. Divide the fruit evenly between the jars, layering it on top of the chia mixture. Sprinkle 1 tablespoon of the coconut chips on top of each fruit layer. Use a long spoon to dig right in, or screw the lid onto each jar for a breakfast to go.

½ cup unsweetened nut milk, coconut milk, soy milk, or dairy milk

2 tablespoons chia seeds

3 teaspoons maple syrup

2 dashes of pure vanilla extract

2 cups diced mango, whole blueberries, or stemmed and sliced strawberries, or a combination

2 tablespoons toasted coconut chips

CINNAMON-APPLE OATMEAL OVERNIGHT JARS

Once you get the hang of the basic method, you can experiment with using fresh berries or diced fruit in place of the applesauce and a different spice in place of the cinnamon. Topping each jar with a dollop of plain yogurt just before serving is tasty and delivers an extra nutrient boost.

1 **MAKE THE OATMEAL**

Have ready 2 pint jars with lids. In each jar, layer the following in order: ½ cup oats, 2 tablespoons applesauce, ½ teaspoon cinnamon, 2 tablespoons nuts, and 1–2 teaspoons honey. Pour 1 cup of the milk into each jar, screw on the lids, and refrigerate for at least 4 hours or up to 3 days.

2 **FINISH & SERVE THE OATMEAL**

Remove the lids and enjoy chilled, or cover loosely with a paper towel and microwave on high for 1 minute to enjoy warm. Stir well before eating.

1 cup old-fashioned rolled oats

4 tablespoons applesauce

1 teaspoon ground cinnamon

4 tablespoons chopped toasted pecans, walnuts, or hazelnuts

2–4 teaspoons honey or other sweetener

2 cups unsweetened nut milk, coconut milk, soy milk, or dairy milk

YOGURT PARFAIT BREAKFAST POPS

A great grab-and-go option for busy school mornings, this frozen breakfast comes with plenty of nutrients—strawberries are packed with vitamin C, manganese, fiber, and antioxidants—to keep you on track for the day. Mango makes a nice alternative to the strawberries. Use fresh or thawed frozen mango cubes and purée them in a blender with the honey before adding them to the ice pop molds.

1 MIX THE STRAWBERRIES

In a small bowl, combine the strawberries, honey, and lemon juice. Using a fork, toss to mix and crush some of the berries. Let stand for 10 minutes.

2 FILL THE ICE POP MOLD

Have ready a 6-well ice pop mold. Spoon a generous tablespoonful of yogurt into the bottom of each mold. Spoon about 1 tablespoon of the berries over the yogurt in each mold, then top with another generous tablespoonful of yogurt and 1 tablespoon of the granola; push the granola gently into the yogurt with the tip of the spoon so it doesn't fall apart when the pops are unmolded. Insert an ice pop stick into the center of each well. Cover tightly and freeze until firm, at least 2 hours or up to 3 days.

3 UNMOLD THE ICE POPS

To unmold the ice pops, run the molds under hot water just until loosened, then gently but firmly pull the ice pops from the molds. Serve cold.

1 cup strawberries, stemmed and sliced

1 tablespoon honey

½ teaspoon fresh lemon juice

1¼ cups vanilla whole-milk Greek yogurt

½ cup granola, homemade (page 31) or store-bought

>> EGGS ADD A PROTEIN BOOST that's hard to beat in the morning. To make sure no bits of shell end up in your eggs, crack each egg into a small bowl and check for shell fragments before slipping it into the hot pan.

FRIED EGG BREAKFAST BURRITO

Bell pepper, beans, avocado, and a fried egg make up a hefty morning dish that's full of flavor and nutrients to help you start your day. Headed out the door? Wrap the warm burrito in aluminum foil or waxed paper, slip it into your backpack, and then when you're ready to take a bite, fold back the wrapping and enjoy.

1 COOK THE VEGETABLES

In a large frying pan over medium heat, warm 1 tablespoon of the oil. Add the onion and bell pepper and cook, stirring occasionally, until tender, about 5 minutes. Stir in the garlic and cook until fragrant, about 1 minute. Add the beans, stir well, then pour in the water. Simmer until the beans are heated through and the liquid is almost completely evaporated, about 5 minutes. Remove from the heat, season to taste with salt, and keep warm.

2 FRY THE EGGS

In a large frying pan (preferably nonstick) over medium heat, warm the remaining 1 tablespoon oil. One at a time, crack the eggs into the pan. Sprinkle the eggs with salt and pepper. Cover, reduce the heat to medium-low, and cook until the whites begin to set and the yolks thicken, about 2 minutes for sunny-side-up eggs. Using a spatula, flip the eggs over and cook for about 30 seconds for eggs over easy, about 1 minute for eggs over medium, and about 1½ minutes for eggs over hard. Remove the pan from the heat.

3 ASSEMBLE THE BURRITOS

Place a warm tortilla on a work surface. Using the spatula, carefully transfer an egg to the center of the tortilla. Top the egg with one-fourth of the bean mixture, 2 avocado wedges, and 2 tablespoons of the pico de gallo. Fold the edge of the tortilla nearest you over the filling, then fold in both sides. Starting again at the edge nearest you, roll up the tortilla to enclose the filling. Repeat with the remaining ingredients to make 4 burritos total. Serve warm.

2 tablespoons olive oil

½ cup chopped yellow onion

½ cup chopped red bell pepper

1 clove garlic, minced

1 can (15½) black beans or pinto beans, drained and rinsed

½ cup water

Kosher salt and freshly ground pepper

4 large eggs

4 flour tortillas, each about 9 inches in diameter, warmed

1 ripe avocado, halved, pitted, peeled, and cut into 8 wedges

½ cup Pico de Gallo (page 122) or store-bought salsa of choice

SPINACH, BACON & EGG MUFFIN CUPS

You can bake these easy egg muffin cups up to 4 days in advance and store them in an airtight container in the refrigerator. Then, when you want a quick snack, pop one into the microwave.

1 PREHEAT THE OVEN

Preheat the oven to 375°F. Spray 12 standard muffin pan cups with cooking spray.

2 THAW THE SPINACH

Rinse the frozen spinach in a colander under cold running water for 10–20 seconds, then let it thaw while you cook the bacon.

3 COOK THE FILLING

Line a plate with paper towels. In a frying pan over medium heat, fry the bacon, stirring often, until lightly browned on the edges, 3–4 minutes. Using a slotted spoon, transfer the bacon to the towel-lined plate. Pour off all but 1 tablespoon of the bacon fat in the pan. Return the pan to low heat, add the green onion, and cook, stirring, for 1 minute. Add the onion to the plate with the bacon.

4 ASSEMBLE THE CUPS

In a bowl, whisk together the eggs and milk until blended. Squeeze the spinach dry with your hands and add to the egg mixture. Add the cheese, bacon, and green onion. Stir gently until mixed.

5 BAKE THE CUPS

Using a ladle, divide the egg mixture evenly among the prepared muffin cups. Bake until the egg cups are puffy and set, 20–22 minutes. Let cool in the pan on a wire rack for at least 5 minutes, then turn them out onto the rack. Serve warm or at room temperature.

Nonstick cooking spray for the cups

1 cup loosely packed frozen spinach leaves (about one-fourth 10-oz package)

4 slices turkey bacon, thinly sliced crosswise

2 tablespoons thinly sliced green onion

8 large eggs

¼ cup milk

¾ cup shredded Monterey jack cheese

BLUEBERRY-QUINOA MUG MUFFIN

The perfect last-minute breakfast, this filling, gluten-free muffin is cooked in the microwave in under 5 minutes. With options for types of sweetener, milk, and fat, you can customize the ingredients to suit your taste.

1 MAKE THE BATTER

Put the butter into a microwave-safe mug, place the mug in the microwave, and microwave on high until melted, 1–1½ minutes. Remove the mug from the microwave. Add the milk and vanilla and mix well with a fork. Add the sugar, baking powder, salt, cinnamon, and flour and stir with the fork just until evenly mixed. Using a rubber spatula, fold in the blueberries.

2 MICROWAVE THE MUFFIN

Return the mug to the microwave and microwave on high until puffed and a toothpick inserted into the muffin comes out clean, 1½–2 minutes. Check after 1½ minutes and add more time in 10-second intervals, if needed. Let cool slightly before eating.

2 tablespoons unsalted butter or coconut oil

3 tablespoons whole dairy milk, unsweetened almond milk, or coconut milk

¼ teaspoon pure vanilla extract

2 tablespoons granulated or coconut sugar

¼ teaspoon baking powder

¼ teaspoon salt

Pinch of ground cinnamon

¼ cup quinoa flour

3–4 tablespoons fresh or frozen blueberries

CARROT-APPLE MUFFINS

A box grater makes easy work of grating carrots and apples in minutes. Be sure to hold it securely with one hand, work slowly, and keep your fingers away from the sharp grates. Make a batch of these healthy muffins on Sunday and bring them to school for snacks during the week.

1 PREHEAT THE OVEN

Preheat the oven to 400°F. Line 12 standard muffin cups with paper liners.

2 MAKE THE BATTER

In a bowl, whisk together the all-purpose flour, whole wheat flour, oat bran, brown sugar, baking powder, baking soda, salt, cinnamon, and chia seeds. Set aside. In a large bowl, using an electric mixer, beat the eggs on low speed until blended, then beat in the yogurt and butter until well mixed. Add the flour mixture and mix on low speed just until combined. The batter will be very thick and slightly dry. Using a rubber spatula or wooden spoon, mix in the apple and carrot just until evenly distributed. Do not overmix or the muffins will turn out tough.

3 BAKE THE MUFFINS

Using a large ice cream scoop, fill each prepared muffin cup about three-fourths full. If using the topping, in a small bowl, stir together the turbinado sugar and cinnamon. Sprinkle the topping on the batter in each muffin cup, dividing it evenly. Bake until a toothpick inserted into the center of a muffin comes out clean, 16–18 minutes. Let cool in the pans on wire racks for about 5 minutes, then turn out the muffins onto the racks to cool. Serve at room temperature. Store leftover muffins in an airtight container at room temperature for up to 3 days.

⅔ cup all-purpose flour

⅔ cup whole-wheat flour

¼ cup oat or wheat bran

½ cup firmly packed light brown sugar

1½ teaspoons baking powder

½ teaspoon baking soda

½ teaspoon salt

1 teaspoon ground cinnamon

2 tablespoons chia seeds

2 large eggs

1 cup plain whole milk Greek yogurt

4 tablespoons unsalted butter, melted and cooled

1 cup peeled and grated tart apple, such as Granny Smith (about 1 large apple)

1 cup peeled and grated carrot (about 2 carrots)

FOR THE TOPPING (OPTIONAL)

2 tablespoons turbinado sugar

1 teaspoon ground cinnamon

SEIZE-THE-DAY SMOOTHIES

Learn to make great smoothies by blending up these four delicious recipes, then experiment with your own favorite ingredient combinations. Substituting fruits or yogurt flavors is a good place to start. You can also add some protein powder for a satisfying post-soccer-practice energy boost, or a handful of spinach leaves or other nutrient-dense ingredient to help you focus in the classroom. Each shake recipe makes 1–2 servings.

BANANA-DATE PROTEIN SHAKE

MIX THE SMOOTHIE
In a blender, combine the ice, banana, dates, almond butter, almond milk, and cacao powder, if using. Blend until smooth. Pour the smoothie into 1 or 2 glasses and serve right away.

3 or 4 ice cubes

1 banana, peeled and broken into chunks

2 pitted Medjool dates

2 tablespoons almond butter

½ cup unsweetened almond milk

1 tablespoon raw cacao powder (optional)

MANGO SMOOTHIE

MIX THE SMOOTHIE
In a blender, combine the ice, mango, banana, yogurt, and orange juice. Blend until smooth. Pour the smoothie into 1 or 2 glasses and serve right away.

3 or 4 ice cubes

2 cups frozen mango cubes

1 banana, peeled and broken into chunks

¾ cup vanilla low-fat yogurt

1 cup fresh orange juice

GREEN JULIUS

MIX THE SMOOTHIE

In a blender, combine the ice, spinach, oranges, banana, and almond milk. Blend until smooth. Pour the smoothie into 1 or 2 glasses and serve right away.

3 or 4 ice cubes

1 cup firmly packed spinach leaves

2 oranges, peeled and divided into segments

½ banana, peeled and broken into chunks

½ cup unsweetened almond milk or coconut water

VERY BERRY FLAXSEED

MIX THE SMOOTHIE

In a blender, combine the ice, banana, berries, yogurt, grapes, flaxseed, and coconut water. Blend until smooth. Pour the smoothie into 1 or 2 glasses and serve right away.

3 or 4 ice cubes

1 banana

2 cups frozen mixed berries

½ cup vanilla low-fat yogurt

½ cup seedless red grapes

1 teaspoon ground flaxseed

1 cup coconut water

HEALTHY-ISH BANANA BREAD

Makes
1
loaf

Greek yogurt keeps this classic quick bread moist, and very ripe banana gives it a natural sweetness. For a little crunch, scatter ½ cup chopped pecans or walnuts over the top of the batter just before putting the loaf in the oven.

1 PREHEAT THE OVEN

Preheat the oven to 350°F. Butter a 9 x 5-inch loaf pan.

2 MAKE THE BATTER

In a medium bowl, whisk together the all-purpose flour, whole-wheat flour, baking soda, and salt. Set aside. In a large bowl, using an electric mixer, beat together the butter and sugar on medium speed until light and fluffy, about 3 minutes. Add the eggs, one at a time, beating well after each addition. On low speed, add the flour mixture and beat just until combined. Add the bananas, yogurt, and vanilla and beat on low speed just until mixed.

3 BAKE THE BREAD

Pour the batter into the prepared pan and smooth the top with a rubber spatula. Bake until golden brown and a toothpick inserted into the center comes out clean, 50–55 minutes. Check the bread after 30 minutes. If the top is already brown, cover with aluminum foil and return to the oven to finish baking. If the top is not brown at 30 minutes, check again at 40 minutes and cover with foil then, if needed. Let cool in the pan on a wire rack for 20 minutes, then turn out the bread onto the rack, turn the bread upright, and let cool completely. Store leftover bread in an airtight container at room temperature for up to 4 days.

½ cup unsalted butter, at room temperature, plus more for the pan

¾ cup all-purpose flour

¾ cup whole-wheat flour

1 teaspoon baking soda

1 teaspoon salt

½ cup sugar

2 large eggs

1 cup very ripe mashed bananas (about 2 large bananas)

¾ cup plain low-fat or whole milk Greek yogurt

2 teaspoons pure vanilla extract

GOOD-FOR-YOU PUMPKIN BREAD

This updated version of the quick bread classic calls for coconut oil and maple syrup, making it a healthy on-the-go breakfast or afternoon snack. Keep it plain and simple, or add your favorite mix-in, such as chocolate chips, nuts, or raisins.

1 PREHEAT THE OVEN

Preheat the oven to 350°F. Grease two 8½ x 4½ x 2½-inch or 9 x 5 x 3-inch loaf pans with coconut oil.

2 MAKE THE BATTER

In a medium bowl, whisk together the all-purpose flour, whole-wheat flour, sugar, baking soda, cinnamon, nutmeg, and salt. In a large bowl, whisk the eggs until frothy. Add the pumpkin, applesauce, maple syrup, coconut oil, and water and whisk until combined. Make sure all of the oil has been absorbed. Using a rubber spatula, gently fold in the flour mixture just until no traces of flour are visible. Do not overmix. Fold in the mix-in of choice, if using.

3 BAKE THE BREADS

Divide the batter evenly between the prepared pans. Bake until golden brown and a toothpick inserted into the center of a loaf comes out clean, 50–60 minutes. Check the loaves after 40 minutes, and if the tops are starting to get dark, cover them with aluminum foil and return to the oven to finish baking. Let cool in the pans on wire racks for 20 minutes, then turn out the breads onto the racks, turn the breads upright, and let cool completely. Store leftover bread in an airtight container at room temperature for up to 4 days.

½ cup coconut oil, melted and cooled, plus more for the pans

2⅓ cups all-purpose flour

1 cup whole-wheat flour

¾ cup sugar

2 teaspoons baking soda

2 teaspoons ground cinnamon

1½ teaspoons ground nutmeg

1½ teaspoons salt

4 large eggs

1 can (15 oz) pumpkin purée (not pumpkin pie filling)

¼ cup unsweetened applesauce

½ cup maple syrup

1 cup water

1 cup mix-ins, such as mini chocolate chips, chopped nuts, or raisins (optional)

AÇAI SMOOTHIE BOWLS

Small, round, and deep purple-blue, açai berries are the fruits of the açai palm tree of South and Central America. They are loaded with good-for-you antioxidants, vitamin C, and fiber, which make this smoothie bowl an excellent way to begin your day. You won't find fresh açai berries in your local market, but frozen açai berry purée packs in the same great nutrients.

1 MAKE THE SMOOTHIE
In a blender, combine the berry purée, raspberries, and coconut water and blend until smooth.

2 ASSEMBLE THE BOWLS
Divide the smoothie between 2 shallow bowls. Arrange the banana, mango, and kiwifruit slices decoratively on top. Sprinkle with the granola, goji berries, and shredded coconut, drizzle with the honey, and serve.

4 packets (3 oz each) frozen açai berry purée

¼ cup frozen raspberries

½ cup coconut water or apple juice

1 banana, peeled and sliced

1 mango, pitted, peeled, and sliced

2 kiwifruits, peeled and sliced, or 6 strawberries, stemmed and sliced

⅓ cup granola, homemade (page 31) or store-bought

2 tablespoons dried goji berries

2 tablespoons unsweetened shredded coconut

1 tablespoon honey

>> RED-ORANGE GOJI berries, which are native to China, boast many of the same nutrients as açai berries. Add any of your favorite toppings to these wholesome bowls.

NUT & SEED WAFFLES

These crisp, wholesome waffles—a mix of wheat flour, buckwheat, oats, walnuts, and sesame and poppy seeds—are a great way to kick off the day. For a burst-of-flavor finish, warm 1 cup blackberries or blueberries in 2 cups maple syrup for serving with the waffles.

1 PREHEAT THE WAFFLE IRON

Preheat a standard square or round waffle iron. If you want to keep the waffles warm until serving time, preheat the oven to 200°F.

2 MAKE THE BATTER

In a large bowl, whisk together the all-purpose flour, oats, buckwheat flour, baking powder, salt, and sugar. Stir in the walnuts, sesame seeds, and poppy seeds. In a medium bowl, whisk together the buttermilk, eggs, and almond extract until well blended. Pour the liquid ingredients over the dry ingredients and stir with the whisk just until combined and no lumps remain. Stir in the butter.

3 COOK THE WAFFLES

Lightly coat the grids of the waffle iron with cooking spray. Ladle about ½ cup of the batter (or the amount recommended by the manufacturer) onto the lower grid; it should spread to within ½ inch of the edge. If needed, use the back of a wooden spoon to smooth it toward the edge. Close the lid and cook until steam is no longer visible or a light on the iron indicates the waffle is ready. Carefully open the lid and serve right away or transfer to a sheet pan and keep warm in the oven. Repeat with the remaining batter, stirring the batter each time before scooping out more and spraying the grids with more cooking spray if needed to prevent sticking.

4 SERVE THE WAFFLES

Serve the waffles warm. Pass the maple syrup at the table.

¾ cup all-purpose flour

⅓ cup old-fashioned rolled oats

¼ cup buckwheat flour

1 tablespoon baking powder

¼ teaspoon salt

3 tablespoons firmly packed light brown sugar

¼ cup chopped walnuts

1 tablespoon sesame seeds

1½ teaspoons poppy seeds

1½ cups low-fat buttermilk

3 large eggs

¼ teaspoon pure almond extract

3 tablespoons unsalted butter, melted and cooled

Nonstick cooking spray for the waffle iron

Maple syrup, warmed, for serving

BERRY & ALMOND GRANOLA

This basic granola recipe makes it easy to create super-tasty, nutty, seedy, fruity granola at home. Make it your own by swapping in your favorite ingredients. Try pecans in place of the almonds, dried cranberries or raisins instead of the strawberries, or puffed rice cereal rather than coconut.

1 PREHEAT THE OVEN

Preheat the oven to 350°F. Line 2 sheet pans with parchment paper.

2 MIX THE GRANOLA

In a large bowl, combine the oats, almonds, coconut, sesame seeds, sugar, salt, cinnamon, and nutmeg. In a small bowl, whisk together the oil and extract. Pour the oil mixture over the oat mixture and stir to coat evenly. Then pour the egg white over the oat mixture and toss and stir gently to mix evenly. Pour half of the mixture onto each prepared pan and spread it evenly.

3 BAKE THE GRANOLA

Bake the granola, stirring it once or twice, until nicely toasted, about 35 minutes. Remove from the oven and let cool. Stir in the berries just before serving or storing. Store in an airtight container at room temperature for up to 1 month.

2½ cups old-fashioned rolled oats

1 cup sliced almonds

½ cup unsweetened flaked coconut

½ cup sesame seeds or sunflower seeds

⅓ cup lightly packed light brown sugar

¾ teaspoon salt

¾ teaspoon ground cinnamon

¼ teaspoon ground nutmeg

½ cup coconut oil or canola oil

1 teaspoon pure almond extract

1 large egg white, beaten until frothy

1 cup freeze-dried or dried strawberries, blueberries, blackberries, or cherries

SOUPS & SALADS

VEGETABLE-PASTA SOUP WITH PESTO DRIZZLE

Feel free to swap out or add whatever vegetables you like to this soup. To help you decide what changes you might want to make, visit your local farmers' market and check out the season's bounty. Sugar snap peas, mushrooms, and cauliflower are just a few of the possibilities.

1 COOK THE ONION & TOMATOES

In a frying pan over medium heat, warm the oil. Add the onion and cook, stirring occasionally, until softened and translucent, about 5 minutes. Add the tomatoes and their juice and cook, stirring, until the tomatoes are tender, about 8 minutes. Remove from the heat.

2 SIMMER THE SOUP

In a large saucepan, combine the broth, tomato mixture, carrots, potatoes, leeks, and celery. Bring to a boil over high heat, reduce the heat to medium-low, and simmer gently for 15 minutes. Add the green beans, zucchini, pasta, and white beans and simmer until the vegetables and pasta are tender, about 10 minutes.

3 SERVE THE SOUP

Ladle the soup into individual bowls and top each serving with a dollop of pesto. Serve right away.

1 tablespoon canola oil

1 yellow onion, chopped

1 can (14 oz) diced tomatoes with juice

8 cups reduced-sodium chicken broth

4 carrots, peeled and thinly sliced

2 Yukon gold potatoes, diced

2 leeks, white parts only, thinly sliced

2 large celery ribs with leaves, thinly sliced

4 oz green beans, trimmed and cut into 1-inch pieces (about 2 cups)

1 zucchini or yellow summer squash, sliced

1 cup small pasta shells, fusilli, or other small shape

1 cup drained canned white beans, rinsed

Basil Pesto, homemade (page 122) or store-bought

BUTTERNUT SQUASH & APPLE SOUP

Vary this tasty weeknight soup by adding a different garnish every time. Try a swirl of Greek yogurt, a sprinkling of toasted almonds, or a dash of chili powder.

1 COOK THE VEGETABLES

In a large saucepan over medium heat, melt the butter. Add the onion and cook, stirring occasionally, until softened and translucent, about 8 minutes. Add the garlic and cook, stirring, until fragrant, about 1 minute. Add the squash, apples, and 5 cups broth, raise the heat to high, and bring to a boil. Reduce the heat to low, cover, and simmer until the squash is very tender, about 20 minutes.

2 PURÉE THE SOUP

Remove from the heat. You can purée the soup using an immersion blender or a stand blender. To use an immersion blender, let the squash mixture cool slightly, submerge the end of the blender stick in the soup, and blend, moving the stick around the pan, until the mixture is smooth. To use a stand blender, let the squash mixture cool to lukewarm. Then, working in batches, transfer the soup to the blender and blend until smooth. Pour each batch into a large bowl until all the soup is puréed, then return all the soup to the saucepan. (If the soup is too thick, add as much of the remaining 1 cup broth as needed to achieve a good consistency.)

3 MAKE THE CROUTONS (IF USING)

In a frying pan over medium heat, melt the butter with the oil. Add the bread pieces and cook, stirring often, until lightly browned, about 4 minutes. Remove from the heat.

4 SERVE THE SOUP

Season the soup to taste with salt and pepper. Ladle into individual bowls, top with the croutons (if using), and serve.

2 tablespoons unsalted butter

1 yellow onion, halved and sliced

2 cloves garlic, minced or pressed

1 butternut squash (about 4 lb), halved, seeded, peeled, and cut into big chunks (see Tip)

2 tart green apples, peeled, cored, and cut into chunks

5–6 cups reduced-sodium vegetable or chicken broth

Salt and freshly ground pepper

FOR THE CROUTONS (OPTIONAL)

2 tablespoons unsalted butter

1 tablespoon olive oil

2 thick slices sourdough French bread, torn into small pieces

» SAFETY TIP

To make the squash easier to cut, soften it in the microwave: Cut a thick slice from the top and bottom of the squash, poke all over with a fork, then microwave on high for 3½ minutes.

EASY TOMATO SOUP

This tomato soup is perfect in its simplicity. Parmesan crisps add a salty, cheesy finish, but you can swap them for a sprinkling of chopped fresh basil, if you like.

1 MAKE THE CRISPS

Preheat the oven to 350°F. Line a sheet pan with aluminum foil. Spread the cheese over the foil in a thin, even layer. Bake until golden brown and crisp, about 10 minutes. Remove from the oven and let cool on the pan. The cheese will continue to crisp as it cools.

2 COOK THE VEGETABLES

Meanwhile, begin making the soup: In a large saucepan over medium heat, warm the oil and butter. Add the onion and cook, stirring often, until softened, 5–7 minutes. Add the garlic and cook, stirring, for 2 minutes. Add the tomatoes and their juice and the broth, raise the heat to high, and bring to a boil. Reduce the heat to medium-low and simmer, stirring occasionally, for 20 minutes.

3 PURÉE THE SOUP

Remove the pan from the heat. You can purée the soup using an immersion blender or a stand blender. To use an immersion blender, let the tomato mixture cool slightly, submerge the end of the blender stick in the soup, and blend, moving the stick around the pan, until the mixture is smooth. To use a stand blender, let the soup cool to lukewarm. Then, working in batches, transfer the soup to the blender and blend until smooth. Pour each batch into a large bowl until all the soup is puréed, then return all the soup to the saucepan.

4 REHEAT & SERVE THE SOUP

Return the saucepan to medium-low heat. Stir well, then season to taste with salt and pepper. Heat, stirring, until a steady stream of steam rises from the surface. Ladle the soup into individual bowls. Using a thin spatula, lift the sheet of crisp cheese from the pan and break it into 6 pieces. Garnish each bowl with a crisp and serve.

FOR THE PARMESAN CRISPS
1 cup freshly shredded Parmesan cheese

FOR THE SOUP
1 tablespoon olive oil

2 tablespoons unsalted butter

1 yellow onion, coarsely chopped

2 cloves garlic, minced

1 can (28 oz) diced tomatoes with juice

4 cups reduced-sodium chicken or vegetable broth

½ teaspoon salt

½ teaspoon freshly ground pepper

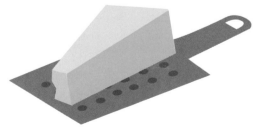

» IF POMEGRANATES ARE OUT OF SEASON, use chopped cashews or hazelnuts in place of the seeds or double the amount of sliced almonds.

Makes
4
servings

FRUITY, NUTTY KALE & QUINOA SALAD WITH POMEGRANATE

This gluten-free salad boasts a healthy mix of kale and quinoa, which together provide plenty of protein and fiber to give you energy for hours, plus the pomegranate seeds deliver a hefty dose of vitamin C.

1 COOK THE QUINOA

In a small saucepan, combine the quinoa, water, and salt and bring to a boil over high heat. Reduce the heat to low, give the quinoa a stir, cover, and cook, without lifting the lid, until the liquid is absorbed and the quinoa is tender, about 15 minutes. Remove from the heat and let stand, covered, for 5 minutes. Uncover and fluff with a fork, then cover and let cool to room temperature.

2 MAKE THE VINAIGRETTE

While the quinoa cools, make the vinaigrette. In a small jar with a lid, combine the lemon juice, vinegar, and oil. Cover and shake until evenly blended. Season to taste with salt and pepper.

3 ASSEMBLE THE SALAD

In a large bowl, combine the quinoa, kale, carrots, pomegranate seeds, mint, almonds, and sesame seeds and toss to mix evenly. Just before serving, add the avocado and vinaigrette and toss gently to coat all the ingredients evenly with the vinaigrette.

FOR THE SALAD

1 cup quinoa, rinsed

2 cups water or reduced-sodium chicken broth

½ teaspoon salt

2 cups baby kale

2 small carrots, thinly sliced

¼ cup pomegranate seeds

2 tablespoons fresh mint leaves

2 tablespoons toasted sliced almonds or roasted sunflower seeds

1 tablespoon sesame seeds

½ avocado, peeled and sliced

FOR THE VINAIGRETTE

2 tablespoons fresh lemon juice

1 tablespoon white wine vinegar

¼ cup extra-virgin olive oil

Salt and freshly ground pepper

Soups & Salads **39**
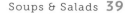

CHINESE CHICKEN SALAD

Crunchy and packed with flavor, this salad is rich in vitamins thanks to all the vegetables and mandarin oranges, and full of protein thanks to the chicken and almonds. If all the delicious components of this dish start making you hungry before it's ready, set aside extra bean sprouts for munching on while you work.

1 COOK THE CHICKEN

Put the chicken into a small saucepan or sauté pan in a single layer. Add just enough broth to cover the chicken. Cover the pan and bring to a boil over high heat. Reduce the heat to low and simmer until the chicken is opaque throughout when cut into with a knife, 10–15 minutes. Using tongs, transfer the chicken to a plate and let cool. Discard the broth or save for another use. When the chicken is cool enough to handle, using your fingers, shred it into bite-size pieces.

2 MAKE THE DRESSING

While the chicken cooks, make the dressing: In a small bowl, stir together the teriyaki sauce, safflower oil, mayonnaise, vinegar, sesame oil, and ginger.

3 ASSEMBLE & SERVE THE SALAD

In a salad bowl, combine the salad greens, cucumber, snow peas, and bean sprouts and toss gently with the tongs. Scatter the chicken evenly over the top, then sprinkle with the almonds and the orange slices, if using. Drizzle the dressing over the salad. Using the tongs or a large fork and spoon, gently toss the salad until evenly coated with the dressing. Divide the salad evenly among 4 salad plates. Sprinkle each serving with the rice noodles, if using, then serve.

FOR THE CHICKEN

2 small skinless, boneless chicken breast halves (about 8 oz each)

About 2 cups reduced-sodium chicken broth

FOR THE DRESSING

2 tablespoons teriyaki sauce

1 tablespoon safflower oil

1 tablespoon mayonnaise

1 tablespoon rice vinegar

1 teaspoon Asian sesame oil

1 teaspoon peeled and grated fresh ginger

4 cups mixed baby greens

½ English cucumber, peeled, halved lengthwise, and cut into half-moons

1 cup snow peas, trimmed

1 cup bean sprouts

1 tablespoon toasted sliced almonds

⅓ cup drained canned mandarin orange slices (optional)

About ¼ cup fried rice noodles (optional)

BROCCOLI-APPLE LUNCH BOX SLAW

This tangy-sweet slaw is the perfect remedy for the two o'clock after-lunch slump. The broccoli, apple, and avocado add a wealth of micronutrients, while the Greek yogurt and nuts provide healthy fats and protein. Working together, they will keep you feeling full and energized for the rest of your day.

1 MAKE THE DRESSING

In a bowl, using a fork, mash the avocado until smooth. Add yogurt, lemon juice, and mustard and stir until well blended. Season to taste with salt and pepper.

2 ASSEMBLE THE SLAW

In a large bowl, combine the broccoli slaw, apple, and cranberries and toss to mix well. Add the dressing and toss until the broccoli and fruits are evenly coated.

3 FINISH & SERVE THE SLAW

Transfer the slaw to a serving plate, top with the cashews, and serve.

FOR THE DRESSING

1 avocado, halved, pitted, and peeled

2 tablespoons plain whole-milk or low-fat Greek yogurt

2 tablespoons fresh lemon juice

1 teaspoon Dijon mustard

Salt and freshly ground pepper

FOR THE SLAW

1 package (6 oz) broccoli slaw

½ large Honeycrisp apple, cored and diced

½ cup dried cranberries or currants

½ cup roasted cashews, chopped

VEGGIE & RICE NOODLE SALAD

A spiralizer makes quick work of transforming raw vegetables into long, curly "noodles." To keep the recipe gluten-free, check the rice noodle package, as some brands contain wheat flour. Brown rice pasta is another good choice.

1 MAKE THE VINAIGRETTE

In a large bowl, whisk together the lemon juice, oil, salt, pepper, and sugar to make a vinaigrette. Set aside.

2 MAKE THE VEGETABLE NOODLES

Set up the spiralizer, fitting it with the fine shredder blade. Trim off both ends of the carrots, zucchini, and beet. Peel the carrots and beet. Following the manufacturer's instructions, spiralize the carrot into long, round, thin strands, stopping to break or cut the strands every 3–4 rotations. Repeat with the zucchini and beet. (If you don't have a spiralizer, you can use a julienne peeler.) When cutting the zucchini, cut only the outer part, rotating the zucchini a quarter turn each time you reach the seedy center. Discard the center seedy portion or reserve for another use. Add the vegetable noodles to the vinaigrette in the bowl and toss to mix.

3 BOIL THE RICE NOODLES

Bring a large pot of water to a boil over high heat. Add the rice noodles to the boiling water and stir gently. Cook until the noodles are al dente, according to the package directions. Drain in a colander, rinse with cold water, and let drain in the sink for 5 minutes.

4 ASSEMBLE THE SALAD

Add the rice noodles to the vegetable noodles and toss together gently until everything is evenly coated with the vinaigrette. Sprinkle with the almonds, toss briefly to mix, and serve.

FOR THE VINAIGRETTE

2 tablespoons fresh lemon juice

2 tablespoons extra-virgin olive oil

1 teaspoon salt

½ teaspoon freshly ground pepper

Pinch of sugar

FOR THE SALAD

2 large carrots

1 large zucchini or yellow summer squashes

1 yellow or red beet

7 oz rice noodles, preferably linguine size

2 tablespoons lightly toasted sliced almonds

CHICKEN-TORTILLA SOUP

Use store-bought cooked chicken or cook it yourself in advance (page 122) and this popular soup can be ready in under 20 minutes. Add chopped tomato or canned black beans for a boost of flavor and chunkier texture.

1 MAKE THE SOUP BASE & PREP THE GARNISHES

In a large saucepan, warm the oil over medium heat. Add the onion and cook, stirring, until translucent, about 3 minutes. Add the chili powder and stir until fragrant, about 1 minute. Pour in the broth and bring to a boil. While the broth is heating, put the tortilla chips, cheese, avocado, and cilantro in small individual bowls and set the bowls on the table.

2 FINISH & SERVE THE SOUP

Add the chicken to the broth, adjust the heat to a simmer, and simmer until the chicken is heated through, about 3 minutes. Season to taste with the lime juice and salt. Ladle into soup bowls and serve, allowing everyone to add garnishes as desired.

FOR THE SOUP

1 tablespoon olive oil

½ yellow onion, finely chopped

2 teaspoons chili powder

6 cups reduced-sodium chicken broth

2 cups cooked shredded chicken, store-bought or homemade (page 122)

Juice of 3–4 limes

Salt

FOR GARNISH

1½ cups broken tortilla chips

½ cup crumbled queso fresco or shredded Monterey jack cheese

1 avocado, halved, pitted, peeled, and cubed

¼ cup chopped fresh cilantro

» TOAST PUMPKIN SEEDS in a large, dry frying pan over medium heat, tossing and stirring with a wooden spoon for about 3 minutes until they begin to "pop" and start to turn golden brown. Turn off the heat, transfer the seeds to a plate, and let cool before serving.

RAINBOW CARROT RIBBON SALAD

Rich in vitamin A, carrots come in a rainbow of colors—purple, red, orange, yellow, and white—and any combination will work for this salad. You will need a sturdy vegetable peeler to cut them into pretty ribbons.

1 MAKE THE CARROTS RIBBONS

Place a carrot flat on a work surface. Holding the top end of the carrot with one hand, use a vegetable peeler to "peel" thin strips off the carrot lengthwise. As you work, rotate the carrot to peel it evenly. Stop making the ribbons when the center of the carrot is too thin to hold steady. Transfer the ribbons to a large bowl or plate. Repeat with the remaining carrots.

2 ASSEMBLE THE SALAD

Put the lettuce on the bottom of a large bowl. Arrange the cucumber slices on top, followed by the carrot ribbons. Set aside.

3 MAKE THE DRESSING

In a bowl, whisk together the yogurt, mayonnaise, buttermilk, lemon juice, dill, parsley, and salt. Taste and add more salt if needed.

4 DRESS & SERVE

If you will be serving all of the salad in one sitting, pour about 1 cup of the dressing over the salad, then, using 2 large spoons, toss it with the vegetables, coating them evenly. Sprinkle the pumpkin seeds on top and serve the remaining dressing alongside. Alternatively, you can serve portions of the salad in small salad bowls, pour a few tablespoons of the dressing on top of each portion, and then sprinkle some pumpkin seeds on top. Leftover undressed salad and dressing can be packed into separate airtight containers and stored in the refrigerator for up to 3 days.

1 lb rainbow carrots (about 8), peeled

1 head red or green leaf lettuce or romaine lettuce, cored and chopped

1 English or Persian cucumber, sliced

½ cup pumpkin seeds, toasted

FOR THE DRESSING

½ cup plain whole-milk or low-fat Greek yogurt

½ cup mayonnaise

⅓ cup low-fat buttermilk

2 tablespoons fresh lemon juice

1 tablespoon chopped fresh dill

1 tablespoon chopped fresh flat-leaf parsley

½ teaspoon salt

FAJITA SALAD WITH SALSA VINAIGRETTE

A Tex-Mex favorite, fajitas—"little belts" in Spanish—are traditionally grilled strips of skirt steak wrapped up in soft flour tortillas. Here, that same tasty beef is turned into a healthy salad with the addition of lettuce, tomatoes, peppers, onions, beans, and avocado and a topping of crunchy tortilla chips.

1 MAKE THE VINAIGRETTE

In a small jar with a lid, combine the salsa, vinegar, and lime juice. Add 4 tablespoons of the oil, cover, and shake until mixed. Taste and add up to 2 tablespoons more oil if needed. Set aside.

2 PREPARE THE STEAK, PEPPERS & ONIONS

Heat a stove-top grill pan over medium-high heat. Meanwhile, evenly drizzle 1 tablespoon of the oil over both sides of the steak and rub it into the meat. Then sprinkle both sides with salt and pepper. Cut each bell pepper in half lengthwise and remove the stem, seeds, and ribs. Place the bell pepper halves on a plate. Trim the root end and tough green tops off of each green onion and add the onions to the plate with the peppers. Drizzle the peppers and onions with the remaining 1 tablespoon oil and toss to coat evenly.

FOR THE VINAIGRETTE

1 tablespoon mild tomato salsa

1 tablespoon red wine vinegar

2 teaspoons fresh lime juice

4–6 tablespoons extra-virgin olive oil

3 GRILL THE STEAK, PEPPERS & ONIONS

Place the steak on the hot grill pan and cook, using tongs to turn once, until well grill-marked on both sides, about 4 minutes per side for medium-rare. Transfer the meat to a plate and set aside. Add the peppers and onions to the grill pan and cook, turning with tongs as needed to color evenly, until nicely browned and tender, about 5 minutes. Transfer the peppers and onions to the plate with the steak. When the onions and peppers are cool enough to handle, transfer them to a cutting board. Cut the onions into thin slices and the peppers into narrow strips. Transfer the steak to the cutting board and cut across the grain into ½-inch-wide strips.

4 ASSEMBLE THE SALADS

Divide the lettuce, tomatoes, beans, onions, peppers, and avocado evenly among 4 shallow salad bowls and toss to combine. Top each salad with one-fourth of the steak. Spoon the vinaigrette over the salads, dividing it evenly. Top with tortilla chips and serve.

» IF THE WEATHER IS GOOD, take this recipe outdoors. Ask an adult to help you prepare a charcoal or gas grill for direct grilling over medium-high heat for cooking the steak, peppers, and onions.

FOR THE SALAD

1 lb skirt steak

2 tablespoons extra-virgin olive oil

Salt and freshly ground pepper

1 green bell pepper

1 red bell pepper

4 green onions, root ends trimmed

½ head iceberg lettuce, shredded

3 plum tomatoes, diced

1 cup drained canned black or pinto beans, rinsed

1 avocado, halved, pitted, peeled, and diced

Tortilla chips for topping

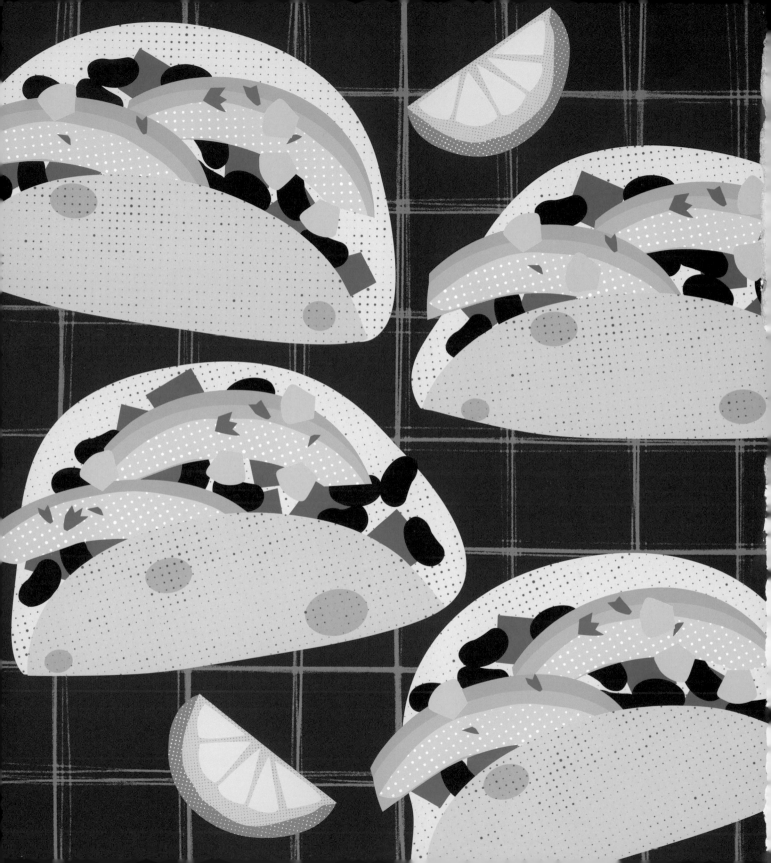

MAINS

CHICKEN, BROCCOLI & CASHEW STIR-FRY

A stir-fry comes together fast, so always have all of your ingredients prepped and ready to go before you begin cooking. A wok spatula, with its shovel-like shape, or a wooden spoon, is ideal for stirring and tossing the ingredients in the hot pan.

1 MARINATE THE CHICKEN

In a large bowl, whisk together 1½ teaspoons of the soy sauce, the vinegar, and ¼ teaspoon of the cornstarch, dissolving the cornstarch. Season with salt and pepper and add the chicken. Toss the chicken in the marinade and let stand at room temperature for 10 minutes.

2 MAKE THE OYSTER SAUCE MIXTURE

In a cup, whisk together the broth, oyster sauce, and the remaining 1½ teaspoons soy sauce and ¼ teaspoon cornstarch. Set aside.

3 COOK THE BROCCOLI

Fill a saucepan with water and bring to a boil over high heat. Add a big pinch of salt and the broccoli and cook until the broccoli is tender-crisp, about 3 minutes. Drain in a colander in the sink and set aside.

4 COOK THE CHICKEN

Heat a wok or a large nonstick frying pan over high heat. When the pan is very hot, add the chicken and all its marinade and toss and stir until the chicken is opaque throughout, about 6 minutes. Stir in the ginger and garlic and cook, stirring, for 30 seconds. Stir the oyster sauce mixture, add it to the pan, and let simmer, stirring once or twice, until the sauce thickens, about 2 minutes.

5 FINISH & SERVE THE STIR-FRY

Stir in the cashews and broccoli and stir and toss just until heated through, about 30 seconds. Serve with the rice. Pass the hot sauce at the table, if using.

3 teaspoons reduced-sodium soy sauce

1 teaspoon rice vinegar

½ teaspoon cornstarch

Salt and freshly ground pepper

½ lb boneless, skinless chicken breasts, cut into ½-inch cubes

2 tablespoons reduced-sodium chicken broth or water

1 tablespoon oyster sauce

½ lb broccoli, trimmed and cut into small florets

1 tablespoon peeled and minced fresh ginger

1 clove garlic, minced

2 tablespoons cashews

Steamed rice (page 123) for serving

Hot pepper sauce for serving (optional)

SWEET POTATO TACOS WITH BLACK BEANS, CORN & AVOCADO

These all-vegetable tacos are packed with so much flavor you won't even notice there's no meat. The sweet potato is the star here, but it's surrounded by plenty of nutrient-rich supporting players. Add some Pico de Gallo (page 122), if you wish.

1 BAKE THE SWEET POTATO

Preheat the oven to 425°F. Pile the sweet potato in the center of a rimmed baking sheet. Drizzle with 2 tablespoons of the oil and toss to coat evenly. Sprinkle with the chili powder and season with salt and pepper and toss again to coat evenly. Spread the sweet potato in a single layer. Bake the sweet potato, stirring once halfway through the baking time, until tender, about 15 minutes.

2 WARM THE TORTILLAS

Wrap the tortillas in aluminum foil and place in the oven about 5 minutes before the sweet potato is ready. After the sweet potato is removed, turn off the oven and leave the tortillas in the oven to stay warm until ready to use.

3 PREPARE THE BEANS

Meanwhile, in a frying pan over medium heat, warm the remaining 1 tablespoon oil. Add the onion and cook, stirring occasionally, until translucent, about 5 minutes. Add the garlic and cook, stirring often, for 1 minute longer. Stir in the cumin and coriander, then add the beans and stir until heated through, 1–2 minutes.

4 ASSEMBLE & SERVE THE TACOS

Unwrap the tortillas and place 2 tortillas on each of 4 plates. Top each tortilla with one-eighth each of the sweet potato, beans, corn, avocado, cheese, and cilantro and finish with a squeeze of lime juice. Fold the tortillas in half to make tacos and serve right away.

1 large sweet potato or yam, about 1¼ lb, peeled and cut into ½-inch dice

3 tablespoons olive oil

Big pinch of chili powder

Salt and freshly ground pepper

8 corn tortillas, each about 8 inches in diameter

½ small yellow onion, finely chopped

1 clove garlic, minced

½ teaspoon ground cumin

¼ teaspoon ground coriander

1 can (14½ oz) black beans, drained and rinsed

¾ cup frozen corn, thawed and drained

½ avocado, peeled and cut into 8 slices

½ cup crumbled feta cheese

½ cup chopped fresh cilantro leaves

2 limes, halved

FISH IN A PACKET WITH TOMATOES & BASIL

Here is a tasty protein-forward main course that's so easy to make you can put it together on a school night. All the flavors of this simple fish dish are trapped inside neat foil packets, which release a wonderful aroma when opened at the table.

1 ASSEMBLE THE PACKETS

Preheat the oven to 375°F. Have ready four 12-inch squares of aluminum foil. Lay a piece of foil in front of you. Crisscross 2 green onion halves on half of the foil. Lay a piece of fish on top of the onions. Arrange 2 or 3 basil leaves over the fish. Top with 6 cherry tomato halves, cut side down, and a few olive slices, if using. Drizzle a little olive oil over the fish and sprinkle with salt and pepper. Fold the uncovered half of the foil over the fish and crimp all the edges to seal. Repeat to make 3 more packets.

2 BAKE & SERVE THE PACKETS

Put the fish packets on a rimmed baking sheet. Bake for 15 minutes. Remove the pan from the oven. Holding a packet by its ends, transfer it to a plate. Work carefully, as the middle of the packet is hot! Cut a slit into the top with scissors or unfold the edges to reveal the fish. To check if the fish is cooked, flake it with a fork. The flesh should appear opaque. If it is translucent, return all the packets to the oven for 1–2 minutes longer. Serve right away with lemon wedges. Warn your guests to watch out for the hot steam as they pull the packets open with their fork and knife.

4 green onions, white part and 2 inches of green, halved lengthwise

4 fish fillets, such as flounder, sole, or red snapper, each 5–6 oz

8–12 fresh basil leaves

12 cherry tomatoes, halved

¼ cup sliced black olives, preferably Kalamata (optional)

Olive oil, as needed

Salt and freshly ground pepper

Lemon wedges for serving

CHICKPEA COCONUT CURRY WITH CARROTS & GINGER

Chickpeas are a great source of plant-based protein and other nutrients. Here they are turned into a creamy, hearty vegetarian curry with the addition of coconut milk. Serve with warm naan or steamed rice (page 123), if you like.

1 COOK THE ONION, CARROT & SEASONINGS

In a large saucepan set over medium-high heat, warm the oil. Add the onion and carrot and cook, stirring occasionally, until the vegetables start to soften, about 5 minutes. Add the garlic and ginger and cook, stirring, until fragrant, 1 minute. Add the curry powder, salt, and pepper and stir to combine.

2 MAKE THE CURRY

Add the coconut milk, broth, chickpeas, and chard and stir to combine. Bring to a simmer, stirring occasionally, then reduce the heat to medium. Cook until the chard is wilted and the carrots are soft, about 10 minutes. Stir in the sugar.

3 SERVE THE CURRY

Taste and adjust the seasoning with salt and pepper if needed. Ladle into individual bowls, sprinkle with cilantro (if using), and serve.

1 tablespoon coconut oil or olive oil

1 yellow onion, diced

3 carrots, peeled, halved lengthwise, and cut into ¼-inch-thick half-moons

3 cloves garlic, minced or grated

2-inch piece fresh ginger, peeled and grated

2 teaspoons yellow curry powder

1 teaspoon salt

Big pinch freshly ground pepper

2 cans (13½ oz each) full-fat coconut milk

2 cups reduced-sodium vegetable or chicken broth

1 can (15 oz) chickpeas, drained and rinsed

1 bunch Swiss chard or kale, stemmed and chopped

1½ teaspoons granulated or coconut sugar

Fresh cilantro leaves for serving (optional)

SPAGHETTI SQUASH PIZZA BOWLS

When you shred cooked spaghetti squash with a fork, it looks just like spaghetti.
That means this recipe delivers two favorites in one bowl: spaghetti and pizza!

1 PREHEAT THE OVEN & PREPARE THE BAKING SHEET

Preheat the oven to 400°F. Line a large, rimmed baking sheet with parchment paper.

2 CUT THE SQUASHES IN HALF

Ask an adult for help with this step. On a cutting board, using a large, sharp knife, cut off about 1 inch from both ends of each squash. Stand 1 squash upright on the cutting board and carefully cut the squash in half lengthwise. Scoop out and discard the seeds and fibers. Repeat with the second squash. Drizzle the cut surface of each half with 1 tablespoon of the oil, then sprinkle with salt and pepper. Place the halves, cut side down, on the prepared baking sheet.

3 BAKE THE SQUASH HALVES

Bake the squash until the flesh is golden brown and easily pierced with a fork, 45-50 minutes. Let cool on the pan on a wire rack until cool enough to handle, 10-15 minutes. Then, using a fork and starting at one end of a squash half, scrape the flesh lengthwise to create strands that look like spaghetti. Repeat with the remaining halves.

4 FINISH THE BOWLS

Top the squash strands in each half with ¼ cup of the Parmesan cheese and sprinkle with salt and pepper. Pour ½ cup of the marinara sauce onto each half. Use the fork or a spoon to mix together the squash, Parmesan, and sauce. Top each half with ½ cup of the mozzarella. Return the baking sheet to the oven and bake until the cheese is melted and starting to brown, 15-20 minutes. Let cool on the pan on the wire rack until cool enough to handle, 10-15 minutes. Sprinkle with more Parmesan cheese and with the basil, if using, and serve.

2 spaghetti squashes (about 3 lb each)

4 tablespoons olive oil

Salt and freshly ground pepper

1 cup freshly grated Parmesan cheese, plus more for serving

2 cups marinara or other tomato sauce

2 cups shredded part-skim mozzarella cheese

Fresh basil leaves for serving (optional)

BEEF & GREEN BEAN STIR-FRY

Flank steak is a lean protein, and green beans are high in vitamins C and K and in fiber, making this easy stir-fry a healthy weeknight choice. Cook the rice while you prepare the stir-fry so both are ready for serving at the same time.

1 PARBOIL THE GREEN BEANS

Bring a saucepan filled with water to a boil over high heat. Have ready a bowl of ice water. Add the beans to the boiling water and parboil for 1 minute. Drain into a colander in the sink, then transfer to the ice water to stop the cooking.

2 MIX THE SAUCE

In a small bowl, stir together the soy sauce, ginger, garlic, green onion, and chile oil (if using).

3 COOK THE BEANS & MEAT

In a wok or large frying pan over high heat, warm 1 tablespoon of the peanut oil, swirling to coat the bottom and sides of the pan. When the oil is very hot but not quite smoking, add the green beans and stir and toss every 10–15 seconds until lightly browned, about 2 minutes. Transfer to a dish. Add another 1 tablespoon peanut oil to the pan over high heat, again swirling to coat the pan. When the oil is hot but not quite smoking, add half of the beef strips and stir and toss every 15–20 seconds until lightly browned but still slightly pink inside, 2–3 minutes. Transfer to a bowl. Add the remaining 1 tablespoon peanut oil to the pan and cook the remaining beef the same way.

4 FINISH & SERVE THE STIR-FRY

Return the first batch of beef to the pan and add the bell pepper. Stir and toss over high heat just until the pepper begins to wilt, 1–2 minutes. Cook, stirring and tossing the mixture occasionally, until the sauce thickens, 1–2 minutes. Return the green beans to the pan and toss to coat with the sauce. Serve right away with the rice.

½ lb green beans, trimmed and cut on the diagonal into 1½-inch pieces (about 1½ cups)

3 tablespoons reduced-sodium soy sauce or tamari

1 teaspoon peeled and finely chopped fresh ginger

1 small clove garlic, minced

1 green onion, finely chopped

½ teaspoon chile oil (optional)

3 tablespoons peanut or vegetable oil

1 lb flank steak, cut in half horizontally and then cut vertically into thin strips

1 red bell pepper, seeded and cut lengthwise into ¼-inch-wide strips

Steamed rice for serving (page 123)

THREE-BEAN VEGETARIAN CHILI

Traditional chili takes on a brand-new look here. Gone are the meat and the long cooking. In their place are colorful bell peppers and three kinds of legumes—black beans, kidney beans, and chickpeas—and less than 15 minutes on the stove.

1 CUT THE BELL PEPPERS
Remove the stems from the bell peppers. Cut the peppers lengthwise into strips, then cut crosswise into squares.

2 COOK THE CHILI
In a large saucepan over medium heat, warm the oil. Add the yellow onion and bell peppers and cook, stirring occasionally, until soft and lightly golden, about 6 minutes. Stir in the garlic, chili powder, oregano, cumin, salt, and red pepper flakes and cook, stirring occasionally, until fragrant, 1–2 minutes. Add the beans, tomatoes and their juice, and cilantro (if using) and cook until the beans and tomatoes are heated through and the flavors have blended, 5–6 minutes.

3 GARNISH & SERVE
Ladle the chili into individual bowls and sprinkle with the cheese and green onions. Serve right away.

2 large green bell peppers, seeded

2 large red bell peppers, seeded

3 tablespoons olive oil

1 yellow onion, chopped

4 cloves garlic, minced

1 tablespoon chili powder

1 tablespoon dried oregano

2 teaspoons ground cumin

1 teaspoon salt

½ teaspoon red pepper flakes

1 can (15 oz) red kidney beans, drained and rinsed

1 can (15 oz) black beans, drained and rinsed

1 can (15 oz) chickpeas, drained and rinsed

1 can (14½ oz) diced fire-roasted tomatoes with their juice

⅓ cup chopped fresh cilantro (optional)

6 tablespoons shredded Monterey jack cheese

2 green onions, including tender green tops, thinly sliced

Makes
4–6
servings

LINGUINE PRIMAVERA

Invented in New York City in the 1970s, linguine primavera—primavera is "spring" in Italian—combines pasta and seasonal fresh vegetables in a colorful, nutrient-rich dish that's finished with a sprinkling of Parmesan.

1 **BLANCH THE VEGETABLES**

Fill a large pot with salted water and bring to a boil over high heat. Have ready a large bowl of ice water. Add the broccoli to the boiling water and boil for 1 minute. Add the asparagus and boil for 1 minute longer. Drain the vegetables into a colander in the sink, then transfer to the ice water to stop the cooking. Drain again and transfer to a bowl. Add the peas and set aside.

2 **COOK THE PASTA**

Fill the pot with salted water again and bring to a boil over high heat. Add the linguine, stir, and cook, stirring occasionally, until al dente, about 8 minutes or according to the package directions. Scoop out about ½ cup of the pasta water and set aside. Drain the pasta into the colander and rinse briefly with cold water. Drizzle with 1 tablespoon of the oil, toss to coat evenly, and set aside.

3 **COOK THE VEGETABLES**

In a large frying pan over medium-low heat, melt the butter with the oil. Add the garlic and cook, stirring often, for 2 minutes. Add the zucchini and cook, stirring, until barely tender, about 2 minutes. Add the broth and ⅓ cup of the pasta water. Bring to a boil over medium-high heat. Stir in the the cream and reserved vegetables. Reduce the heat to medium-low and cook, stirring often, until the vegetables are just tender, about 3 minutes. Stir in the Parmesan.

4 **FINISH & SERVE THE PASTA**

Add the reserved pasta to the frying pan and toss to mix with the sauce and vegetables, adding more pasta water if the sauce seems dry. Stir in the basil. Season to taste with salt and pepper and serve.

1 cup small broccoli florets

1 cup asparagus tips

½ cup frozen peas, thawed

12 oz dried linguine

2 tablespoons olive oil, plus more as needed

1 tablespoon unsalted butter

2 cloves garlic, minced

1 small zucchini, trimmed and thinly sliced

⅓ cup reduced-sodium vegetable broth

½ cup heavy cream

½ cup freshly grated Parmesan cheese

2 tablespoons thinly shredded fresh basil

Salt and freshly ground pepper

» VARY THIS SPRINGTIME RECIPE with your own favorite vegetables. Try adding sliced carrots with the broccoli and sliced yellow or red bell pepper with the peas for a more vibrant and colorful dish.

ZUCCHINI LASAGNA WITH TURKEY BOLOGNESE

You'll get plenty of vitamin A in this lasagna, thanks to the zucchini. You can use a vegetable peeler instead of a knife to cut the zucchini into thin slices. To make this dish gluten-free, use gluten-free lasagna noodles or leave out the noodles and double the amount of zucchini.

1 CUT THE ZUCCHINI

Trim off the ends of each zucchini. Holding a zucchini flat on a work surface, run a vegetable peeler (preferably a serrated one designed for soft vegetables) down the length of the zucchini to peel off a thick strip. Continue to peel strips from the zucchini, stopping to rotate the zucchini 180 degrees when you reach its seedy center. Repeat with the remaining zucchini. Discard the center seedy portions or reserve for another use. Set the zucchini "noodles" in a colander, sprinkle lightly with salt, and set aside while you make the béchamel and Bolognese.

2 MAKE THE BÉCHAMEL

In a small saucepan over low heat, melt the butter. Add the flour and cook, stirring constantly, with a wooden spoon until a thick, smooth paste forms, about 3 minutes. Do not allow to brown. Pour in a little of the hot milk and, using a whisk, stir to loosen the paste a bit. Then slowly pour in the remaining milk while whisking constantly to prevent lumps from forming. Increase the heat to medium-low and cook, stirring often, until slightly thickened, about 5 minutes. Add the Parmesan and stir until melted. Season to taste with salt and pepper. Remove from the heat and set aside.

1½ lb zucchini

Salt

FOR THE BÉCHAMEL

4 tablespoons unsalted butter

3 tablespoons all-purpose flour

1½ cups whole milk, heated until steaming

¾ cup freshly grated Parmesan cheese

Salt and freshly ground pepper

Continued on page 64 »

» *Continued from page 63*

3 **MAKE THE BOLOGNESE**

In a frying pan over medium heat, warm the oil. Add the onion and cook, stirring occasionally, until translucent, about 5 minutes. Add the garlic and cook, stirring, for 1 minute longer. Add the turkey and cook, breaking up the turkey with a wooden spoon, until cooked through, 5–8 minutes. Carefully pour off the fat or spoon it from the pan. Stir in the tomatoes and their juice and cook, stirring often, for 2 minutes. Add the tomato sauce and basil, mix well, and bring to a simmer. Cook, stirring often, until the flavors have melded, about 5 minutes. Remove from the heat and set aside.

4 **ASSEMBLE THE LASAGNA**

Position a rack in the lower third of the oven and preheat the oven to 375°F. Lightly oil a 9 x 13-inch baking dish. Remove the zucchini from the colander and blot dry with paper towels. To assemble the lasagna, spread a thin layer of the Bolognese sauce over the bottom of the dish. Top the sauce with half of the lasagna noodles in a single layer (break them to fit if needed), followed by half of the remaining Bolognese, half of the zucchini, and half of the béchamel. Repeat the layers, using the remaining noodles, Bolognese, zucchini, and béchamel. Sprinkle the final layer of béchamel evenly with the mozzarella.

5 **BAKE THE LASAGNA**

Bake until the noodles and zucchini are tender, the sauce is bubbling, and the mozzarella is golden brown, about 45 minutes. Remove from the oven, let cool for about 5 minutes, then cut into squares and serve hot.

FOR THE BOLOGNESE

1 tablespoon olive oil

½ yellow onion, finely chopped

1 large clove garlic, minced

1 lb ground turkey, preferably dark meat

1 can (14½ oz) diced tomatoes with their juice

3 cups tomato or marinara sauce

½ teaspoon dried basil

Olive oil for the pan

About 6 oz no-boil lasagna noodles

1½ cups shredded part-skim mozzarella cheese

USE A SERRATED KNIFE with a sawing motion to keep the layers of lasagna intact while cutting it.

GREEK SALAD WRAPS WITH TZATZIKI

This is the perfect plan-ahead meal to serve your family on a busy weeknight. You can make the tzatziki or hummus and the salad minus the romaine and cook the chicken a day in advance and refrigerate them. Then, come dinnertime, all you'll need to do is warm the bread, finish the salad, and roll up the wraps.

1 HEAT THE BREADS
Preheat the oven to 400°F. Wrap the breads in aluminum foil and place in the oven to warm for 5 minutes.

2 MAKE THE SALAD
Meanwhile, in a medium bowl, combine the lettuce, cucumber, tomato, olives, cheese, and onion. In a small bowl, stir together the oil and vinegar to make a vinaigrette. Season to taste with salt and pepper. Drizzle the vinaigrette over the salad. Using tongs or 2 large spoons, toss the salad until well mixed.

3 WRAP IT UP
Place four 10-inch squares of aluminum foil on a work surface. Unwrap the breads and place 1 bread on each foil square. Spread 1 tablespoon of the tzatziki evenly over each bread. Top with the salad, dividing it evenly and sprinkling it in a thick layer. Scatter the chicken over the salad (if using), again dividing it evenly. Starting at one side, roll up each wrap, using the foil to hold it together snugly. Serve warm.

» IF USING PITA BREAD, you may prefer to cut the breads in half, split them open, and stuff the breads instead of rolling them.

4 flatbreads, such as lavash, naan, or pita

1 cup chopped romaine lettuce

¼ English cucumber, peeled and chopped

1 plum tomato, chopped

2 tablespoons pitted Kalamata olives, chopped

2 tablespoons crumbled feta cheese

¼ small red onion, thinly sliced

1½ tablespoons olive oil

2 teaspoons red wine vinegar

Salt and freshly ground pepper

¼ cup Tzatziki (page 123) or hummus (page 78)

About 1 cup chopped or shredded Cooked Chicken (page 122), optional

SPAGHETTI WITH CAULIFLOWER PESTO

Not all pesto is made with basil! Here, cauliflower, which is naturally high in fiber and several vitamins, is charred to bring out its nutty flavor and then mixed with parsley, nuts, olive oil, and other ingredients to make a delicious pesto. Use brown rice spaghetti noodles to make this dish gluten-free, if you like.

1 COOK THE CAULIFLOWER
Preheat a stove-top grill pan over high heat. Season the cauliflower florets with salt and pepper. Arrange the cauliflower florets on the hot pan and cook, turning occasionally, until well charred on all sides, 6–8 minutes.

2 MAKE THE PESTO
Turn on a food processor and drop the garlic through the feed tube to finely chop it. Stop the processor and add the parsley, almonds, capers, and oil. Pulse until the mixture is well combined but still coarse. Set aside.

3 COOK THE PASTA
Fill a large pot with salted water and bring to a boil over high heat. Add the pasta, stir, and cook, stirring occasionally, until al dente, about 8 minutes or according to package directions. Drain into a colander in the sink, then transfer to a serving bowl.

4 TOSS THE PASTA WITH THE PESTO & SERVE
Add the pesto and Parmesan to the hot pasta and toss to coat evenly. Serve right away.

1 small head cauliflower, cored and cut into 1-inch florets

Salt and freshly ground pepper

2 cloves garlic

1 cup fresh flat-leaf parsley leaves

½ cup toasted almonds

2 tablespoons capers

1 cup extra-virgin olive oil

1 lb spaghetti (see note)

½ cup freshly grated Parmesan cheese

CHICKEN & PINEAPPLE KEBABS

For a fun, tangy, healthful spin on chicken kebabs, alternate the chicken cubes with pineapple, which is super-high in vitamin C. Feel free to experiment with different flavors: add some chunks of red bell pepper for a sweet and spicy crunch, or red onion for a sharp, bright flavor. Steamed rice (page 123) is a good side dish.

1 HEAT A GRILL PAN

If using bamboo skewers, soak 12–16 skewers in water to cover for at least 15 minutes. Place a stove-top nonstick grill pan over medium-high heat and heat for 2 minutes.

2 MAKE THE BASTING SAUCE

In a small bowl, combine the pineapple juice, oil, soy sauce, sugar, shallot, ginger, and garlic and stir to mix well.

3 ASSEMBLE THE KEBABS

Thread the chicken cubes alternately with the pineapple cubes onto 12–16 skewers, dividing the chicken and pineapple evenly among the skewers. Brush both the chicken and pineapple lightly with oil.

4 COOK THE KEBABS

Brush the kebabs liberally with some of the basting sauce. Grill the kebabs, basting them frequently with the sauce and turning them with tongs as needed, until the chicken and pineapple are lightly browned on all sides and the chicken is opaque throughout, 7–10 minutes. Transfer to a platter and serve at once.

½ cup pineapple juice

3 tablespoons olive oil, plus more for brushing

2 tablespoons reduced-sodium soy sauce

2 tablespoons firmly packed light brown sugar

1 tablespoon minced shallot

1 tablespoon peeled and grated fresh ginger

1 clove garlic, finely minced

1 lb boneless, skinless chicken breasts, cut into 1-inch cubes

½ pineapple, peeled, cored, and cut into 1-inch cubes

» GRILL THE KEBABS on an outdoor grill,
if you prefer. Ask an adult to help you prepare a
charcoal or gas grill for direct grilling over medium-
high heat. Brush the grill grate clean and then oil
the grate before placing the kebabs on top.

HOW TO MAKE
INSIDE-OUT VEGGIE SUSHI

1

Using water-moistened fingers, spread the seasoned rice in an even layer over the nori. Sprinkle evenly with sesame seeds.

2

Place a piece of plastic wrap over the rice, then place a bamboo mat over the plastic. Flip the nori and mat together so the nori is on top.

3

Arrange some of the veggies in rows over the bottom third of the nori sheet.

4

Roll the uncovered bottom edge of the nori over the veggies for one full turn, gently pressing it into a roll.

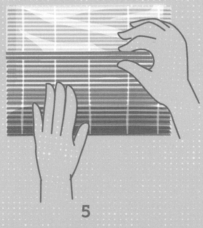

5

Pull the bottom of the plastic-lined bamboo mat up over the roll to help roll it up, pressing gently while rolling.

6

Remove the mat and plastic wrap. Using a knife moistened in water, cut each roll into 8 equal pieces.

INSIDE-OUT VEGGIE SUSHI

Thin slices of cucumber, carrot, and avocado are always a hit in these fun rolls. But use your imagination and add any thinly sliced vegetables you like. If you don't have a Japanese bamboo sushi mat, a sturdy kitchen towel will work too. Sticky rice is sticky business, so have a bowl of water nearby to help make it easier to handle.

1 COOK THE RICE

Place the sushi rice in a strainer and rinse well under running cold water until the water runs clear. Transfer the rice to a saucepan and stir in the water. Set the saucepan over medium-high heat and bring to a boil. Reduce the heat to low, cover, and cook until all the water is absorbed, about 15 minutes.

2 MAKE THE RICE SEASONING

Meanwhile, in a small saucepan over low heat, combine the vinegar, sugar, and salt and heat, stirring, until the sugar and salt dissolve, about 2 minutes. Remove from the heat and let cool completely.

3 SEASON THE RICE

When the rice has finished cooking, using a rubber spatula, scoop it out into a large baking dish and spread it out evenly. While gently slicing through the rice with the spatula, slowly pour the vinegar mixture evenly over the rice. Then flip the rice with the spatula to mix in the vinegar mixture evenly. Do not stir the rice or you will crush the grains. Cover the dish with a clean kitchen towel and let cool to room temperature before using.

FOR THE SEASONED RICE

1 cup short-grain white rice

2 cups water

3 tablespoons rice vinegar

2 tablespoons sugar

¾ teaspoon salt

FOR THE ROLLS

4 nori sheets, each about 8 x 7 inches

2 tablespoons toasted sesame seeds (white, black, or a combination)

½ English cucumber, peeled and cut into matchsticks

1 medium carrot, peeled and cut into matchsticks

1 ripe avocado, halved, pitted, peeled, and thinly sliced

Reduced-sodium soy sauce and/or pickled ginger for serving (optional)

Continued on page 72 »

» *Continued from page 71*

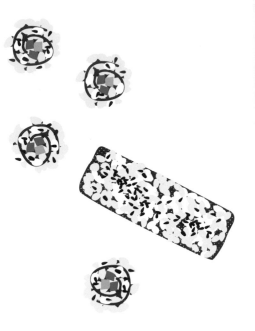

4 ASSEMBLE THE ROLLS

Fill a small bowl with water. Lay 1 piece of nori, shiny side down and with a shorter side facing you, on a clean, dry work surface. Scoop about ½ cup of the seasoned rice onto the nori. Dip your fingers into the bowl of water and spread the rice in a thin even layer over the nori. Add a little more rice, if necessary, to cover the sheet. Sprinkle the rice evenly with 1½ teaspoons of the sesame seeds. Place a sheet of plastic wrap loosely over the rice, then place a bamboo sushi mat (or sturdy kitchen towel) on top of the plastic. Place one hand underneath the nori and the other on top of the mat (towel) and carefully flip the stack over so the nori is on the top, keeping the shorter side facing you. Leaving a 1-inch border uncovered on the edge of the nori nearest you, arrange about one-fourth each of the cucumber sticks, carrot sticks, and avocado slices horizontally in a single row across the bottom third of the nori sheet. Using the plastic wrap and mat (towel) to help, roll the uncovered edge of nori closest to you over the vegetables for one full turn. Be careful not to let the plastic wrap or mat (towel) get tucked inside the roll. Pause and use the mat (towel) to help tighten the roll. Gently pull the plastic wrap and mat (towel) off the roll slightly, then use them to rotate the roll for another full turn. Repeat until the roll is completely rolled up. Use the mat (towel) to tighten the roll and tuck in any filling or rice that might have fallen out of the ends. Remove the plastic wrap and mat (towel) and transfer the roll, seam side down, to a cutting board. Repeat with the remaining nori, rice, and vegetables.

5 CUT & SERVE THE ROLLS

Dip a sharp chef's knife into the bowl of water and slice each roll in half horizontally. Slice each half into 4 equal pieces for a total of 8 pieces, dipping your knife into the bowl of water after each slice. Transfer to a serving plate. Serve with bowls of soy sauce and pickled ginger alongside, if desired.

TURKEY MEATLOAF

Meatloaf doesn't always look pretty, but it sure can taste delicious! Here, the classic ground beef has been traded out in favor of ground turkey, which has a slightly lower saturated fat content than ground beef of the same leanness. If you end up with leftovers, remember just two words: meatloaf sandwiches.

1 **PREHEAT THE OVEN & PREPARE THE PAN**
Preheat the oven to 350°F. Lightly oil a small roasting pan.

2 **MAKE THE MEAT MIXTURE**
In a large bowl, combine the turkey, onion, bread crumbs, ½ cup of the ketchup, the eggs, Worcestershire sauce, salt, and pepper and mix with clean hands just until evenly combined. Transfer the mixture to the prepared pan and shape it into a thick loaf about 9 inches long and 5 inches wide.

3 **BAKE & SERVE THE MEATLOAF**
Bake the meatloaf for 45 minutes. Remove from the oven, spread the top with the remaining 3 tablespoons ketchup, and return to the oven. Continue to bake until an instant-read thermometer inserted into the center of the loaf registers 165°F, about 15 minutes longer. Remove from the oven and let stand in the pan for 5 minutes. Using a large, wide spatula, transfer the meat loaf to a serving plate. Cut into slices and serve hot.

Canola oil for the pan

2 lb ground turkey, preferably dark meat

1 yellow onion, minced

½ cup dried bread crumbs

½ cup plus 3 tablespoons ketchup

2 large eggs, lightly beaten

2 tablespoons Worcestershire sauce

1 teaspoon salt

½ teaspoon freshly ground pepper

VIETNAMESE LETTUCE WRAPS

These healthy lettuce wraps are low in calories and fat and high in vitamins and flavor. Plus, they are fun to make and to eat at the table. If you can't find lemongrass, just leave it out. The meatballs will still be tasty without it.

1 **PREHEAT THE OVEN**
Preheat the oven to 375°F. Lightly spray a rimmed baking sheet with cooking spray. Line the pan with aluminum foil and spray the foil.

2 **MAKE THE MEATBALLS**
Cut off and discard the root end and the grassy tops of the lemongrass. Remove the tough outer leaves from the bulb portion to reveal a pale yellow interior. Using a meat pounder or the bottom of a heavy pan, pound the lemongrass four or five times. Finely chop the lemongrass and add it to a large bowl. Chop about half of the cilantro and mint leaves and add to the bowl along with the chicken, garlic, fish sauce, and salt. Stir gently to mix well. Form the mixture into 16 golf ball-size meatballs and place on the prepared pan. Sprinkle the meatballs evenly with the sugar. Bake until lightly browned and cooked through, 15-20 minutes. Transfer to a bowl.

3 **PREPARE THE REMAINING INGREDIENTS**
Meanwhile, ready the remaining ingredients. Fill a small saucepan with water and bring to a boil over high heat. Add the noodles, remove from the heat, and let stand until tender, about 5 minutes. Meanwhile, put the carrot, cucumber, peanuts, and whole herb leaves into separate small bowls. Put the lettuce leaves on a plate. Drain the rice noodles and put them into another small bowl.

4 **SERVE THE LETTUCE WRAPS**
Set the lettuce, vegetables, herbs, nuts, noodles, and meatballs on the table. For each lettuce wrap, invite diners to fill a lettuce leaf with a few meatballs and the remaining ingredients as desired. Dip the lettuce wraps into the dipping sauce, if using, before eating.

Nonstick cooking spray

1 lemongrass stalk

⅓ cup fresh cilantro leaves

⅓ cup fresh mint leaves

1 lb ground chicken or turkey (preferably dark meat)

1 large clove garlic, minced

2 tablespoons Asian fish sauce

¼ teaspoon salt

1 teaspoon sugar

2 oz dried rice vermicelli noodles

1 cup shredded or spiralized carrot

½ English cucumber, thinly sliced

¼ cup chopped roasted peanuts

8 whole red leaf, butter, or iceberg lettuce leaves

Vietnamese Dipping Sauce (page 123), optional

SNACKS

HUMMUS WITH ROOT CHIP DIPPERS

Makes about
3
cups

Thinly sliced root vegetables make crisp and healthy dippers. Other vegetables, such as zucchini and cucumbers, will also work well. This hummus recipe is a classic, perfect with pita wedges or added to a sandwich or wrap (see page 66).

1 **CUT THE CHIPS**

Fill a large bowl with ice water. In a food processor fitted with a thin slicing blade, slice the radishes, carrots, and beet, working with one type of vegetable at a time. As the "chips" are cut, transfer them to the ice water. Let the vegetables stand in the water for at least 20 minutes, or cover and refrigerate for up to 1 day.

2 **MAKE THE HUMMUS**

In a food processor, combine the chickpeas, lemon juice, tahini, oil, garlic, cumin, and salt. Process until a soft, creamy paste forms. Taste and adjust the seasoning with salt and lemon juice if needed.

3 **SERVE THE HUMMUS & CHIPS**

Transfer the hummus to a serving bowl. Drain the root chips, pat dry with a paper towel, and arrange along the edge of the hummus. Serve right away.

FOR THE ROOT
VEGETABLE CHIPS

2 watermelon radishes, peeled

2 large rainbow carrots, peeled

1 small golden beet, peeled

FOR THE HUMMUS

2 cans (15 oz each) chickpeas, drained and rinsed

½ cup fresh lemon juice, plus more if needed

½ cup tahini

3 tablespoons extra-virgin olive oil

5 cloves garlic, minced

¼ teaspoon ground cumin

¾ teaspoon salt

RAINBOW PINWHEELS

Makes
18
pinwheels

These colorful rainbow roll-ups make the perfect bite-size all-vegetable snack.
To simplify assembly, lay out the vegetables and then get a friend to help you roll
them up in the tortillas. These are best when eaten right away.

1 CUT THE VEGETABLES

Cut the carrot, zucchini, and cucumber into matchsticks. To cut
the matchsticks, cut each vegetable piece lengthwise into ⅛-inch-
thick slices. Lay the slices flat and cut them lengthwise again into
thin matchsticks. You should have about 36 carrot matchsticks,
36 zucchini matchsticks, and 18 cucumber matchsticks. Put them
in separate small bowls, using one bowl for each vegetable.

Cut the bell pepper into 2-inch-wide sections. Trim away any of the
ribs, then cut into narrow, 2-inch-long matchsticks. You should have
about 18 bell pepper matchsticks. Put them in another small bowl.

2 CUT THE TORTILLAS

Trim about ½ inch off two opposite sides of each tortilla to square
them up, then cut each tortilla square into 4 long strips each 1¼–
1½ inches wide. You should have 18 strips.

3 ASSEMBLE THE PINWHEELS

Lay a tortilla strip on a work surface. Spread about 1 teaspoon
cream cheese across the entire strip. On one end, about ½ inch
in from the edge, lay 2 carrot matchsticks, 2 zucchini matchsticks,
1 cucumber matchstick, 1 bell pepper matchstick, and 1 parsley sprig.
Carefully roll the edge of the strip around the vegetable bundle
and then continue rolling to the opposite end of the strip. (If the
end of the strip won't stick to the roll, add a little cream cheese
to "glue" it in place.) Transfer to a platter, standing the pinwheel
on an end. Repeat with the remaining tortilla strips, cream cheese,
vegetables, and parsley, transferring the pinwheels to the platter
as you go. Serve right away.

1 carrot, peeled and cut into
about 2-inch lengths

2-inch piece yellow zucchini

2-inch piece cucumber, peeled

½ red bell pepper, seeded

4½ whole-wheat, purple corn–
wheat, tomato-basil, or spinach
tortillas, each about 6 inches in
diameter

6 tablespoons store-bought
sun-dried tomato, herb, or
chive-onion cream cheese

18 small fresh flat-leaf parsley or
cilantro sprigs, each about
2 inches long

SOFT STRAWBERRY OATMEAL BARS

Strawberry jam is always a favorite—especially homemade—but you can swap it out for any flavor you like. These addictive bars, which are great for breakfast as well as snack time, will get softer as the jam starts to blend with the hearty oat dough.

1 **PREHEAT THE OVEN**
Preheat the oven to 350°F. Butter a 9 x 13-inch baking dish. Line the buttered dish with parchment paper, allowing about 2 inches to hang over the narrow ends of the pan.

2 **MAKE THE DOUGH**
In a food processor, combine the all-purpose flour, whole-wheat flour, sugar, cinnamon, baking soda, salt, vanilla, lemon zest, butter, and water. Pulse a few times until the mixture starts to come together and stick along the sides of the bowl. (Add an additional 1 tablespoon water if the dough is not coming together.) Add the oats and pulse a few times until the oats are chopped and distributed evenly throughout the dough, stopping to scrape down the sides of the bowl with a silicone spatula if needed.

3 **ASSEMBLE THE BARS**
Using your hands, press half of the dough into the bottom of the prepared pan. (Pressing it will help it stick together.) Check the edges and corners to be sure they are flat and even with the rest of the dough. Using an icing spatula or butter knife, spread the jam on top of the dough, leaving a ½-inch border uncovered along all the edges. Pour the remaining dough evenly over the jam layer. Press down lightly with your hands to spread it evenly and help it come together.

4 **BAKE THE BARS**
Bake until the top is golden brown and the jam bubbles, 30–35 minutes. Let cool completely in the pan on a wire rack. Use the overhanging edges of the parchment paper to lift the sheet of layered dough out of the pan. Transfer it to a cutting board and cut into bars.

¾ cup cold unsalted butter, cut into cubes, plus more for the baking dish

1 cup all-purpose flour

⅔ cup whole-wheat flour

¾ cup firmly packed light brown sugar

1 teaspoon ground cinnamon

¼ teaspoon baking soda

½ teaspoon salt

2 teaspoons pure vanilla extract

Grated zest of 1 lemon (about 2 teaspoons)

1 tablespoon water

1⅔ cups old-fashioned rolled oats

1½ cups strawberry jam

Mango Smoothie
(page 24)

»SNACK PARTY

Almond Butter
Energy Bites
(page 84)

Sweet Puffed Brown
Rice Rolls (page 97)

Very Berry
Flaxseed Smoothie
(page 25)

ALMOND BUTTER ENERGY BITES

When you need a healthy, filling portable snack, grab a few of these superpowered, no-bake bites. You can substitute peanut butter for the almond butter, if you like, and choose whichever mix-ins appeal to you. Take the nut butter out of the refrigerator a few minutes before you get started, so it's softer and easier to mix.

1 **MIX THE INGREDIENTS**

In a bowl, combine the oats, ground flaxseed, almond butter, honey, vanilla, and mix-ins. Using a rubber spatula, mix well. Cover the bowl with plastic wrap and refrigerate until the almond butter has set, at least 30 minutes.

2 **SHAPE THE BITES**

Remove the bowl from the refrigerator. To shape each bite, measure a tablespoon of the oat mixture and, using lightly dampened hands, shape it into a ball. As the balls are shaped, transfer them to a large plate or rimmed baking sheet. If a coating is desired, put the cacao nibs into a shallow bowl. Add a few balls and roll them around until evenly coated, then return them to the plate or baking sheet.

3 **CHILL & SERVE**

Place the plate or baking sheet in the refrigerator until the balls are set, 5–10 minutes. Transfer to a serving plate and serve. Store leftover balls in an airtight container in the refrigerator for up to 2 weeks or in the freezer for up to 3 months.

» **TO TOAST SHREDDED COCONUT,** line a rimmed baking sheet with parchment paper and spread the coconut on the prepared pan in a thin, even layer. Bake in a preheated 325°F oven, stirring the coconut halfway through baking, until light golden brown, 7–8 minutes.

1 cup old-fashioned rolled oats

⅓ cup ground flaxseed

⅔ cup almond butter, at room temperature

¼ cup honey

1 teaspoon pure vanilla extract

½ cup mix-ins, such as mini chocolate chips, toasted unsweetened shredded coconut (see Tip), or crushed banana chips, or a combination

¼ cup finely chopped cacao nibs or nuts of choice or toasted unsweetened shredded coconut (optional)

SOY & GINGER-GLAZED EDAMAME

Be sure the edamame are still warm when you toss them with the soy mixture so they will more readily absorb it. Then slide the warm tender beans from their pods with your teeth for a nutrient-rich snack that's high in protein and in folate, which is important for good cell growth.

1 COOK THE EDAMAME

Cook the edamame according to the package directions.

2 MAKE THE SAUCE

Meanwhile, in a frying pan over medium-low heat, warm the oil. Add the garlic and ginger and cook, stirring to prevent burning, until softened, 1–2 minutes. Stir in the soy sauce, water, sugar, and vinegar, raise the heat to medium, and cook, stirring, until reduced slightly, about 1 minute. Remove from the heat.

3 SERVE THE EDAMAME

When the edamame is ready, drain and transfer to the frying pan. Toss well to coat evenly. Sprinkle with the red pepper flakes, pour into a bowl, and serve warm.

1 package (12 oz) frozen edamame in the pod (about 4 cups)

1 teaspoon canola oil

1 small clove garlic, minced

1-inch piece fresh ginger, peeled and minced

2 tablespoons reduced-sodium soy sauce or tamari

2 tablespoons water

1½ tablespoons firmly packed light brown sugar

1 tablespoon rice vinegar

½ teaspoon red pepper flakes and/or toasted sesame seeds

PANKO-CRUSTED VEGETABLE BURGER BITES

Crunchy and delicious, these bite-size burgers are a good way to power up with lots of vitamins and protein. Dunked into a spicy yogurt-tahini sauce, they make especially tasty snacks. The prepared vegetable mixture will keep in the refrigerator for up to 1 day—ideal if you want to prep ahead for a party.

1 COOK THE ONION & MUSHROOM
In a large frying pan over medium heat, warm the oil. Add the onion and cook, stirring occasionally, until starting to sweat, about 2 minutes. Add the mushrooms and cook, stirring occasionally, until golden brown, about 4 minutes longer. (As the mushrooms start to release water, use it to help you scrape up the browned bits on the bottom of the pan.) Remove from the heat and let cool.

2 MAKE THE BURGER MIXTURE
Put the cauliflower into a food processor and pulse a few times until it starts to resemble rice. Add the onion-mushroom mixture, carrot, spinach, cilantro, black beans, tomato paste, paprika, chili powder, salt, and pepper and pulse a few times to mix well. Add the eggs and pulse just until combined. Transfer the mixture to a large bowl. Add ½ cup of the bread crumbs and the quinoa and, using a rubber spatula, stir until well mixed. Cover and refrigerate until the mixture becomes firm enough to shape, about 30 minutes.

3 MAKE THE SAUCE
While the burger mixture chills, make the sauce. In a bowl, combine the yogurt, tahini, garlic, 1 tablespoon of the lemon juice, the salt, pepper, and hot sauce (if using) and stir until well blended. Taste and add more lemon juice, salt, and pepper if needed. Cover and refrigerate until ready to use.

1 tablespoon olive oil

½ yellow onion, diced

½ lb cremini or other brown mushrooms, brushed clean, stemmed, and sliced

2 cups cauliflower florets

1 carrot, peeled and coarsely chopped

1 cup packed baby spinach leaves

½ cup lightly packed fresh cilantro or parsley leaves

1 can (15 oz) black beans, drained, rinsed, and patted dry with a paper towel

1 tablespoon tomato paste

1½ teaspoons smoked paprika

2 teaspoons chili powder

1½ teaspoons salt

½ teaspoon ground black pepper

2 large eggs, lightly beaten

1½ cups panko bread crumbs

1½ cups Steamed Quinoa (page 123)

4

BAKE & SERVE THE BURGER BITES

Preheat the oven to 400°F. Line 2 rimmed baking sheets with parchment paper. Spread the remaining 1 cup bread crumbs onto a plate. Using a small ice cream scoop or a tablespoon, scoop up a little of the mixture, forming it into a ball. Toss and roll the ball in the bread crumbs, coating evenly, then place on a prepared baking sheet. Repeat with the remaining mixture, spacing the balls evenly apart. Bake until golden brown and firm, 35–40 minutes. Let cool slightly on the pans on wire racks. Transfer to a serving platter and serve with the sauce alongside.

FOR THE YOGURT-TAHINI SAUCE

1 cup plain whole-milk Greek yogurt

2 tablespoons tahini

1 clove garlic, minced or grated

1–2 tablespoons fresh lemon juice

1 teaspoon salt

¼ teaspoon freshly ground pepper

1 teaspoon hot sauce, such as Sriracha, Tabasco, or sambal oelek, or to taste (optional)

» TOAST SUNFLOWER SEEDS in a large, dry frying pan over medium heat, tossing occasionally with a wooden spoon, for about 3 minutes until golden brown and fragrant.

APRICOT-SUNFLOWER GRANOLA BARS

These chewy bars are the perfect healthy on-the-go snack. You can add ½ cup of your favorite chopped nuts to the dry mix, or swap out the apricots for cranberries, raisins, or any other dried fruit. Look for wheat germ near the oatmeal in the cereal aisle.

1 PREHEAT THE OVEN & PREPARE THE PAN
Preheat the oven to 350°F. Spray a 9 x 13-inch baking pan with cooking spray.

2 MIX THE INGREDIENTS
In a large bowl, combine the oats, wheat germ, cinnamon, salt, apricots, and sunflower seeds and stir with a silicone spatula. In a small saucepan over medium heat, combine the butter, sugar, almond butter, and maple syrup. Bring to a simmer and cook for 1 minute, stirring constantly with the spatula. Remove from the heat and pour over the oat mixture. Stir with the spatula to mix well. Let cool for 5 minutes. In a small bowl, whisk the egg whites until frothy, about 30 seconds. Add the egg whites to the oat mixture and stir to combine.

3 BAKE & CUT THE BARS
Dump the mixture into the prepared pan, then press firmly with the spatula to create an even layer. Bake until the edges are golden brown and the top is no longer sticky to the touch, 20–25 minutes. Let cool slightly in the pan on a wire rack. Cut into 12 rectangular or 16 square bars, then let cool completely in the pan for 1 hour. Wrap each bar in plastic wrap and store in an airtight container at room temperature for up to 10 days.

Nonstick cooking spray for the pan

2½ cups old-fashioned rolled oats

½ cup wheat germ

1 teaspoon ground cinnamon

½ teaspoon salt

1½ cups chopped dried apricots

½ cup sunflower seeds, toasted or untoasted (see Tip)

½ cup unsalted butter, cut into pieces

½ cup firmly packed light brown sugar

½ cup creamy almond or peanut butter

⅓ cup maple syrup

2 large egg whites

TORNADO SWEET POTATO WITH GARLIC-BUTTER DRIZZLE

Potatoes are a sure bet when it comes to making a delicious snack. They are great at taking on flavors and are an easy way to fulfill your carbohydrate needs, which translate to quick energy for the body and the brain.

1 PREPARE THE POTATO

Preheat the oven to 400°F. Soak a wooden skewer in water for 10 minutes. Meanwhile, poke the potato all over with a fork, then microwave on high for 2-3 minutes until softened. Insert the soaked skewer into one end of the potato and gently push it lengthwise through the center of the potato all the way through the potato until the tip emerges from the opposite end. Holding a sharp knife at a slight angle and starting at one end of the potato, cut down to the skewer and continue cutting while rotating the potato away from you to make spiraled rows about ½ inch apart. Gently fan out the spiral so air can circulate between the slices.

2 SEASON THE POTATO

Put the skewered potato on a plate. In a small microwave-safe bowl, combine the butter and garlic. Microwave on high for 25 seconds to melt the butter. Drizzle the garlic butter all over the potato, using a pastry brush to evenly coat all the slices. Sprinkle the potato all over with the spice blend.

3 BAKE THE POTATO

Place the skewered potato in a small baking dish so the skewer ends rest on the rim of the dish, suspending the potato above the bottom of the dish. Bake until crisped on the outside and tender on the inside, 25-30 minutes. Let cool for about 5 minutes before serving, then serve hot.

1 sweet potato, scrubbed and patted dry

2 tablespoons unsalted butter

1 clove garlic, minced

1 teaspoon savory spice blend, such as Mrs. Dash

KALE CHIPS WITH SEA SALT

Just about everyone knows kale is loaded with health benefits. But not everyone knows how to turn kale into a crispy, salty snack that's just as addictive as potato chips. That you'll learn here. Keep an eye on the oven, as the chips can burn easily. And if a smoky, spicy kick appeals, don't leave out the smoked paprika!

1 PREHEAT THE OVEN & PREP THE KALE

Position 2 oven racks in the center of the oven and preheat the oven to 300°F. Rinse the kale well and blot dry thoroughly with a clean kitchen towel. Tear the leaves from the ribs and discard the ribs. Then tear the leaves into fairly large chip-size pieces.

2 SEASON THE KALE

Put the kale into a large bowl and sprinkle with the oil, smoked paprika (if using), and salt. Using your hands, toss the leaves to coat evenly with the oil and seasoning.

3 BAKE THE KALE

Arrange the leaves in a single layer on 2 rimmed baking sheets. Bake, switching the pans between the racks and rotating them back to front, until the leaves are dry and crisp, about 25 minutes. Serve right away. Kale chips are best eaten within a few hours.

1 bunch curly or dinosaur kale, about ½ lb

2 tablespoons olive oil

¼ teaspoon smoked paprika (optional)

½ teaspoon coarse sea salt

FRUIT ROLL-UPS

In-season ripe fruit is very sweet, so you won't need much agave nectar—a liquid sweetener—for these treats. But if your fruit isn't very sweet to start, taste the fruit purée after blending to see if it needs a little more sweetener. Keep an eye on the fruit when it is cooking on the stove top, as it can burn easily.

1 **PURÉE THE FRUIT**

In a blender, combine the fruit, ½ cup agave nectar, and 2 tablespoons lemon juice if using apples or pears or 1 tablespoon lemon juice if using any other fruit. Blend until smooth. Taste and add more agave nectar, 1 tablespoon at a time, if it is not sweet enough.

2 **COOK THE FRUIT**

Transfer the fruit purée to a saucepan, place over medium-high heat, and bring to a simmer. Reduce the heat to medium-low and cook, stirring occasionally with a silicone spatula and scraping the sides of the saucepan often, until the purée is very thick, 30–35 minutes. While the mixture is cooking, it will become foamy and start to bubble. If the bubbles get too big or the fruit starts to splatter, turn down the heat to low. As the purée thickens, stir more often to prevent it from sticking or burning on the bottom of the pan. Remove from the heat and let cool for 5 minutes.

Continued on page 94 »

1 lb chopped (and peeled, if necessary) fruit, such as apples, pears, peaches, plums, strawberries, blackberries, or raspberries

½–¾ cup agave syrup or honey

1–2 tablespoons fresh lemon juice

» *Continued from page 92*

3 DRY THE FRUIT PURÉE

While the purée is cooling, preheat the oven to 200°F. Line a rimmed baking sheet with a silicone baking mat or nonstick aluminum foil. When the purée has cooled, using an icing spatula, carefully spread it in a very thin layer on the prepared baking sheet, leaving the edges slightly thicker so they don't burn. Bake until the purée is set and no longer sticky, about 3 hours. Check after 2 hours and again after 2½ hours, and if the edges are starting to get very dark, turn off the oven and leave the fruit sheet in the warm oven for another hour until set.

4 MAKE THE ROLL-UPS

Let the fruit cool completely in the pan on a wire rack. Lay a large sheet of waxed paper on a work surface. Peel the cooled fruit sheet off the mat or foil and place it, smooth side down, on the waxed paper. Using scissors, trim off the excess waxed paper. No paper should extend beyond the edge of the fruit sheet. Cut the fruit with the paper lengthwise into strips about 1 inch wide. Holding the waxed paper at the bottom, tightly roll up the fruit strips with the paper into coils. Store the roll-ups in lock-top plastic bags at room temperature for up to 3 days. Carefully peel away the paper before eating.

» **EASY DOES IT** when making fruit roll-ups. Take care to spread the fruit purée in a thin, even layer, then bake it in a low oven to prevent burning, but long enough for it to dry out. The fruit sheet is not ready until it no longer sticks to the silicone baking mat or nonstick aluminum foil lining the baking sheet.

GARDEN FRITTATAS

These bite-size squares of fresh vegetable frittata are delicious served on their own, but they are even tastier wrapped in a small radicchio or lettuce leaf. If you cannot find small leaves, tear larger leaves in half or into thirds.

1 PREHEAT THE OVEN
Preheat the oven to 350°F. Butter 24 mini muffin cups.

2 MIX THE FRITTATA MIXTURE
In a bowl, whisk together the eggs and sour cream until blended. Stir in the carrots, zucchini, lemon zest, chives, and Parmesan.

3 BAKE THE FRITTATAS
Spoon the egg mixture into the prepared muffin cups, dividing it evenly. Bake until puffed and golden, about 15 minutes. Let cool in the pan on a wire rack for 5 minutes, then turn the frittatas out onto the rack. Serve warm or at room temperature, with the radicchio alongside, if using, for wrapping.

Unsalted butter for the muffin cups

4 large eggs

½ cup sour cream

2 carrots, peeled and grated

1 large zucchini, grated

1 teaspoon grated lemon zest

3 tablespoons snipped fresh chives

3 tablespoons freshly grated Parmesan cheese

24 small radicchio or lettuce leaves (optional)

SWEET PUFFED BROWN RICE ROLLS

These rolls are sticky business, so use waxed paper to help you press the gooey crisps onto the baking sheet and roll them into a log. Remove the saucepan from the heat as soon as bubbles form to avoid burning the honey "glue" mixture.

1 **MAKE THE PUFFED RICE MIXTURE**

Put the puffed rice into a bowl. In a saucepan over medium-low heat, combine the oil and honey and heat, stirring until the oil melts, about 1 minute. Add the sugar and salt and continue to heat, stirring constantly, until the sugar is completely dissolved and bubbles start to form, 1–2 minutes. Remove from the heat and carefully pour the honey "glue" over the puffed rice. Using a silicone spatula, toss the puffed rice with the honey mixture until evenly mixed and all the honey mixture is absorbed.

2 **MAKE THE ROLLS**

Place three 18-inch-long pieces of waxed paper on a work surface. Scoop about one-third of the puffed rice onto the center of a piece of waxed paper. Fold the paper over the puffed rice and press it into a log about 15 inches long and about 1½ inches in diameter. Leave the roll covered with the waxed paper and set aside. Repeat with the remaining puffed rice mixture and waxed paper to make 2 more logs. Let stand until firm, about 30 minutes.

3 **CUT THE ROLLS**

Remove the waxed paper and transfer the logs to a cutting board. Using a serrated knife, cut the logs into rolls about 4 inches long. Store in an airtight container at room temperature for up to 3 days.

VARIATION

Apple-Cinnamon: Add ½ teaspoon ground cinnamon with the brown sugar and salt to the "glue" mixture and ½ cup chopped dried apple rings to the bowl of puffed rice.

4 cups puffed brown rice cereal or brown rice crisps

2 tablespoons coconut oil

¼ cup honey

2 tablespoons firmly packed light or dark brown sugar

Pinch of salt

POPCORN 4 WAYS

Popcorn makes an easy snack, whether you like it plain, spiced, herbed, or sweet. It's also a good way to get in a workout, as shaking a heavy-bottomed pan over the stove top takes stamina. Use oven mitts to protect your hands and make sure an adult is nearby if help is needed.

1 POP THE CORN

In a large, heavy-bottomed pan with a tight-fitting lid over medium heat, warm the oil. When the oil is hot, add the popcorn and cover the pan. Leave the pan untouched until you hear the first few pops, then shake the pan and continue to cook, shaking the pan every 20 seconds or so, until the popping slows down to about 1 pop every 3–4 seconds, about 6 minutes. Remove from the heat.

2 SEASON THE POPCORN

Transfer the hot popcorn to a serving bowl and toss the with salt to taste and enjoy it plain, or dress it up with one of the following flavor combinations. Serve right away.

CHILI LIME In a large bowl, stir together 2 tablespoons melted unsalted butter, 1 tablespoon grated lime zest, and 1½ teaspoons chili powder. Add the hot popcorn, toss well, and season with salt.

RANCH In a large bowl, stir together 2 tablespoons each melted unsalted butter and freshly grated Parmesan cheese; ½ teaspoon each onion powder, dried dill, and salt; and ¼ teaspoon garlic powder. Add the hot popcorn and toss well.

MAPLE BACON Before you pop the corn, in a frying pan over medium heat, fry 5 slices bacon, turning once, until crisp, 3–5 minutes. Let drain on paper towels, then crumble into small pieces. Use 2 tablespoons of the bacon fat in place of the canola for popping the corn. In a large bowl, mix the crumbled bacon, 1 tablespoon pure maple syrup, 1 tablespoon Sriracha sauce, and 1 tablespoon melted unsalted butter. Add the hot popcorn, toss well, and season with salt.

2 tablespoons canola oil

½ cup unpopped popcorn

Salt

CRISPY CHICKPEAS

Chickpeas—also known as garbanzo beans—are high in protein and fiber, which means they'll keep you feeling fuller and satisfied for longer. If you like, switch up the seasonings, adding 1 teaspoon garlic powder to the mix or substituting ground turmeric and ginger for the cumin and chili powder.

1 SEASON THE CHICKPEAS

Preheat the oven to 400°F. Spread the chickpeas out on paper towels and pat them dry. Transfer to a bowl, add the oil, and toss to coat evenly. Sprinkle on the cumin, chili powder, and salt and toss to mix evenly. Spread the chickpeas in an even layer on a rimmed baking sheet.

2 ROAST THE CHICKPEAS

Roast the chickpeas, shaking the pan every 10 minutes to ensure they brown evenly, until crispy and lightly browned, 30-40 minutes. Let cool completely on the pan on a wire rack before serving. Store any leftovers in an airtight container at room temperature for up to 5 days.

2 cans (15 oz each) chickpeas, drained and rinsed

1 tablespoon olive oil

2 teaspoons ground cumin

2 teaspoons chili powder or smoked paprika

1 teaspoon salt

DESSERTS

BERRY GALETTE WITH NUT CRUST

The nuts in the crust are a good source of protein, and the berries—especially the strawberries—in the filling are high in vitamin C and fiber and full of antioxidants.

1 MAKE THE PASTRY DOUGH

In a food processor, combine the nuts and about 1 tablespoon of the sugar and pulse until the nuts are finely ground. Add the remaining sugar, the flour, and the salt and pulse a few times to mix well. Scatter the butter over the flour mixture and pulse just until the mixture resembles coarse crumbs. Add the water and pulse until the dough clumps together and begins to form a rough mass. If the dough is too crumbly, add more water, a couple of teaspoons at a time. Flour a work surface and transfer the dough to it. Knead the dough briefly until it comes together. Wrap the dough in plastic wrap and refrigerate for at least 1 hour or up to overnight. Let stand at room temperature for 10 minutes before using.

2 ROLL OUT THE PASTRY

Preheat the oven to 425°F. Line a rimmed baking sheet with parchment paper. On a lightly floured work surface, roll out the dough into a round about 12 inches in diameter and ⅛ inch thick. Fold the dough round in half and then into quarters, transfer it to the prepared pan, and unfold it.

3 MAKE THE FILLING

In a bowl, toss together the raspberries, strawberries, lemon juice, sugar, and flour. Spoon the filling onto the dough round, leaving a 2-inch border uncovered around the edge. Fold the edge of the dough up and over the filling, forming pleats as you work.

4 BAKE THE GALETTE

Bake until the filling is bubbling and the pastry is golden brown, about 25 minutes. Let cool slightly on the pan on a wire rack before serving. Cut into wedges. Serve with frozen yogurt, if using.

FOR THE PASTRY

¾ cup hazelnuts, pecans, or walnuts, lightly toasted

⅓ cup sugar

1⅔ cups all-purpose flour, plus more for the work surface

¾ teaspoon salt

6 tablespoons very cold butter, cut into cubes

3 tablespoons ice water, or as needed

FOR THE FILLING

2 cups raspberries

2 cups strawberries, stemmed

2 tablespoons fresh lemon juice

¼ cup sugar

3 tablespoons all-purpose flour

Vanilla frozen yogurt for serving (optional)

FRUITY YOGURT BITES

Makes
24
bites

Bite-size cups, such as mini muffin cups, small tartlet pans, or candy molds, work best for these easy fruit bites. Use full-fat yogurt in different fruit flavors, pairing them with fruit of the same color or flavor. Mango cubes with mango or peach yogurt, diced kiwifruit with key lime yogurt, raspberries with raspberry yogurt, and strawberries with strawberry yogurt are some tasty combos.

1 **MAKE THE YOGURT BITES**
Line a 24-cup mini muffin pan with foil liners or place twenty-four 1½ to 2-inch tartlet pans on a large rimmed baking sheet. Spoon 1–2 tablespoons yogurt into each prepared muffin cup or tartlet pan. Top each portion with a small piece of fruit.

2 **FREEZE THE YOGURT BITES**
Place the muffin pan or baking sheet in the freezer and freeze until the yogurt is solid, about 1 hour. Serve right away, or cover with plastic wrap and store in the freezer for up to 2 days.

4 containers (6 oz each) full-fat fruit-flavored yogurt of choice

1 cup cut-up fresh fruit of choice (24 pieces)

»» TO UNMOLD the bites from tartlet pans or candy molds, dip the bottom of the pan or mold in hot water to loosen the bites, then use the tip of a knife to lift them out.

DOUBLE-DIPPED STRAWBERRIES

The hardest part of this dessert is finding the most beautiful strawberries and the best-quality chocolate. Look for large, ripe berries that are free of soft spots. Have them at room temperature and perfectly dry before dipping them.

1 MELT THE CHOCOLATE

Put the chocolate and oil in a heatproof bowl and set over (not touching) simmering water in a saucepan. Heat, stirring often with a silicone spatula, until melted and smooth, 5–7 minutes. Remove the pan from the heat, but leave the bowl atop the pan to keep the chocolate warm.

2 DIP THE STRAWBERRIES

Line a rimmed baking sheet with waxed paper. Pour some sprinkles onto a saucer. Holding a strawberry by its green leaves, dip it into the melted chocolate until about three-fourths of the berry is covered. Use the spatula, if necessary, to help coat the strawberry evenly with chocolate. Let the excess chocolate drip back into the bowl, then dip the strawberry into the sprinkles or scatter some over the top. Place the strawberry on the prepared baking sheet. Repeat with the remaining strawberries. When all of the berries have been dipped, place the baking sheet in the refrigerator until the chocolate sets, about 10 minutes.

3 SERVE THE STRAWBERRIES

Transfer the berries to a serving plate. They are best eaten the day they are made. If necessary, cover loosely with waxed paper and store overnight in the refrigerator. Serve at room temperature.

1 cup semisweet chocolate chips

1 tablespoon coconut oil or solid vegetable shortening

1–2 pints large fresh strawberries

Rainbow sprinkles for garnish

CHEWY MAPLE COOKIES

Maple syrup adds a buttery, nutty accent to baked goods. Use only pure maple syrup—not "pancake syrup" or "original syrup"—for these cookies to bring out their rich, fall-inspired flavor.

1 PREHEAT THE OVEN

Preheat the oven to 350°F. Line 2 rimmed baking sheets with parchment paper.

2 MAKE THE DOUGH

In a medium bowl, whisk together the flour, baking soda, salt, ginger, cinnamon, and allspice. In a large bowl, using an electric mixer, beat together the butter and sugar on medium-high speed until light and fluffy, about 3 minutes. Add the egg and beat until combined. Add the maple syrup and beat until smooth, about 1 minute. Stop the mixer and scrape down the sides of the bowl with a rubber spatula. On low speed, add the flour mixture and beat just until combined, about 30 seconds.

3 BAKE THE COOKIES

Using a small ice cream scoop or tablespoon, scoop balls of dough onto the prepared baking sheets, spacing the balls about 2 inches apart. Bake until the edges of the cookies are golden brown, 10–12 minutes. Let the cookies cool on the pans on wire racks for 5 minutes, then, using a metal spatula, transfer the cookies to the racks and let cool completely. Store in an airtight container at room temperature for up to 4 days.

2 cups all-purpose flour

1½ teaspoons baking soda

½ teaspoon salt

1½ teaspoons ground ginger

1 teaspoon ground cinnamon

½ teaspoon ground allspice

½ cup unsalted butter, at room temperature

¾ cup firmly packed light brown sugar

1 large egg

½ cup pure maple syrup

»DESSERT PARTY

Peanut Butter Sandwich Cookies
(page 120)

Chocolate-Almond
Cookies (page 113)

Double-Dipped
Strawberries
(page 106)

GLUTEN-FREE ALMOND CAKE

Almond flour replaces the usual wheat flour in this gluten-free cake. Unless you're looking for a workout with a whisk, use an electric mixer for this batter, as both the egg whites and the egg yolks need vigorous beating.

1 PREHEAT THE OVEN

Preheat the oven to 350°F. Butter a 9-inch cake pan, then line the bottom with parchment paper and butter the paper.

2 BEAT THE EGG YOLKS

First, separate the eggs. Place 2 bowls side by side. Crack an egg along its equator and, holding it over 1 of the bowls, carefully pull apart the shell halves just enough to allow the whites to drip into the bowl while the yolk remains cupped in half of the shell (see illustration). Then drop the yolk into the second bowl. Repeat with the remaining eggs. Add the ¾ cup granulated sugar to the yolks and beat with an electric mixer on medium speed or by hand with a whisk until pale yellow and creamy. Beat in the lemon zest and almond extract, mixing well. Switch to a wooden spoon and stir in the almond flour until well blended. Set aside.

3 PREPARE THE ALMONDS

Scoop 1 teaspoon of the egg whites and 1 teaspoon of the granulated sugar into a small bowl and beat with a fork until frothy. Add the almonds, toss to coat with the egg white mixture, and set aside.

Unsalted butter for the pan

4 large eggs

¾ cup plus 2 teaspoons granulated sugar

¼ teaspoon grated lemon zest

½ teaspoon pure almond or vanilla extract

1 cup almond flour

½ cup sliced almonds

Powdered sugar for dusting

4 **BEAT THE EGG WHITES**

Using a clean whisk or beaters, beat the remaining egg whites by hand or on medium speed until frothy. Add the remaining 1 teaspoon granulated sugar and continue beating by hand or on medium-high speed until stiff peaks form. Using a rubber spatula, stir one-fourth of the whipped egg whites into the yolk mixture to lighten it. Gently fold in half of the remaining egg whites until mixed. Then fold in the remaining egg whites just until no white streaks remain. Pour the batter into the prepared pan and smooth the surface with the spatula.

5 **BAKE THE CAKE**

Bake for 20 minutes. Sprinkle the reserved almonds evenly over the top and continue to bake until the cake is deep golden brown and pulls away from the pan sides, 10–12 minutes longer. Let cool in the pan on a wire rack for 10 minutes. Invert the cake onto the rack and peel off the parchment, then turn the cake right side up and let cool completely.

6 **SERVE THE CAKE**

Transfer the cake to a serving plate. Using a fine-mesh sieve or a sifter, dust the top with powdered sugar just before serving.

CHOCOLATE-ALMOND COOKIES

These gluten-free dark chocolate treats drizzled with white chocolate are like eating a mug of hot chocolate. You can trade out the white chocolate chips for milk or dark chocolate or use any combination of the three.

1 MAKE THE DOUGH

In a bowl, whisk together the flour, cocoa powder, baking powder, and salt. Set aside. In a large bowl, using an electric mixer, beat together the butter and granulated and brown sugars on medium speed until light and fluffy, about 3 minutes. Add the eggs, one at a time, beating well after each addition. Beat in the vanilla and almond extracts. Stop the mixer and scrape down the sides of the bowl with a rubber spatula. On low speed, add the flour mixture and mix just until combined, about 1 minute. Cover the bowl and refrigerate for 20 minutes. Meanwhile, preheat the oven to 350°F. Line 2 rimmed baking sheets with parchment paper.

2 BAKE THE COOKIES

Using a small ice cream scoop or a tablespoon, scoop balls of dough onto the prepared baking sheets, spacing the balls about 2 inches apart. Bake until puffed and the tops are starting to crackle, 12–13 minutes. Let the cookies cool on the pans on wire racks for 5 minutes, then, using a metal spatula, transfer the cookies to the racks and let cool completely.

3 DRIZZLE THE COOKIES WITH CHOCOLATE

Put the white chocolate in a heatproof bowl and set over (not touching) simmering water in a saucepan. Heat, stirring often with a silicone spatula, until melted and smooth, 5–7 minutes. Remove the pan from the heat. Using a spoon, drizzle the white chocolate over the cookies. Let stand until the chocolate sets, about 15 minutes, before serving. Store in an airtight container at room temperature for up to 4 days.

1⅔ cups almond flour

½ cup unsweetened cocoa powder

1½ teaspoons baking powder

½ teaspoon salt

½ cup unsalted butter, at room temperature

½ cup granulated sugar

½ cup firmly packed light brown sugar

2 large eggs

½ teaspoon pure vanilla extract

¼ teaspoon almond extract

½ cup white chocolate chips

CHOCOLATE-DIPPED FRUIT CUP CONES

Few desserts could be simpler than these waffle cones rimmed with chocolate and sprinkles and filled with fresh fruit rather than the traditional ice cream. Use fruit that is small enough to fit into these crisp cookie-like receptacles, such as berries or sliced stone fruit.

1 MELT THE CHOCOLATE

Put the oil and chocolate into a heatproof bowl and set over (not touching) simmering water in a saucepan. Heat, stirring often with a silicone spatula, until melted and smooth, 5–7 minutes. Remove the pan from the heat, but leave the bowl atop the pan to keep the chocolate warm.

2 DIP THE CONES

Line a rimmed baking sheet with parchment paper. Pour some sprinkles onto a saucer. Dip the open end of a cone into the chocolate, covering 1–2 inches of the sides and allowing the excess chocolate to drip back into the bowl. Then dip the rim of the cone into the sprinkles, coating it evenly. Place the dipped cone on the prepared baking sheet. Repeat with the remaining cones. Place the baking sheet in the freezer just until the chocolate sets, about 10 minutes.

3 FILL THE CONES & SERVE

Using a cup measure, scoop ⅓ cup of the fruit mixture into each cone. Serve right away.

1 tablespoon coconut oil or solid vegetable shortening

1 cup semisweet or bittersweet chocolate chips

Rainbow or chocolate sprinkles for garnish

4 waffle or sugar cones

1⅓ cups mixed fresh fruit, such as pitted cherries, raspberries, blueberries, blackberries, stemmed and sliced strawberries, grapes, and/or sliced peaches and plums

KIWI SORBET

This vitamin C–packed sorbet is great in summer when you need a refreshing pick-me-up and during cold season for soothing a sore throat. Make sure you put the container in the freezer before the sorbet begins churning so the sorbet doesn't melt when it hits the container.

1 **MAKE THE SORBET**

Put a 4 cup loaf pan or similar-size container into the freezer. In a blender, combine the 10 chopped kiwifruits, the lime juice, and the agave nectar and blend until smooth. Transfer to an ice cream maker and freeze according to the manufacturer's instructions.

2 **FREEZE THE SORBET**

Spoon the sorbet into the chilled container, cover, and freeze until firm, at least 4 hours or up to overnight.

3 **SERVE THE SORBET**

Scoop the sorbet into bowls and top with the remaining 4 chopped kiwifruits, dividing them evenly.

10 ripe green kiwifruits, peeled and coarsely chopped, plus 4 green kiwifruits, peeled and coarsely chopped, for garnish

1 tablespoon fresh lime juice

½ cup light agave nectar

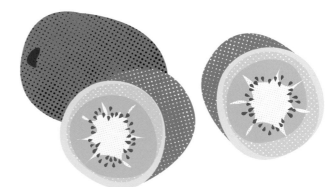

VANILLA-COCONUT BUNDT CAKE

Makes
8–10
servings

Toasting coconut brings out its flavor and adds a nice crunch to the inside and outside of this cake. Be sure to keep an eye on it in the oven, because it can go from white to burned in no time! You can layer it in the middle of the batter for a swirl effect, or whisk it into the flour mixture for crunchy coconut in every bite.

1 **PREPARE THE PANS**

Preheat the oven to 325°F. Spray a 10-inch Bundt pan with baking spray, or coat evenly with room temperature butter and dust with flour. Line a rimmed baking sheet with parchment paper.

2 **TOAST THE COCONUT**

Spread the coconut evenly on the prepared baking sheet. Bake the coconut, tossing it halfway through baking with a wooden spoon or silicone spatula, until light golden brown, 7–8 minutes. Let the coconut cool on the pan on a wire rack for 10 minutes before using. Leave the oven on at 325°F.

3 **MAKE THE BATTER**

Set aside ¼ cup of the coconut milk to use for the glaze. In a medium bowl, whisk together the remaining coconut milk, egg whites, and vanilla until smooth. In a large bowl, whisk together the flour, sugar, baking powder, and salt until blended. Add the butter and, using an electric mixer, beat on medium speed until pea-size crumbs form, about 1 minute. Add half of the coconut milk mixture and beat just until combined. Add the remaining coconut milk mixture and beat just until combined.

FOR THE CAKE

Nonstick baking spray for the pan (optional)

1½ cups sweetened shredded coconut

1 can (13½ oz) full-fat coconut milk

5 large egg whites

1½ teaspoons pure vanilla extract

2½ cups all-purpose flour

1 cup granulated sugar

3 teaspoons baking powder

1¼ teaspoons salt

¾ cup unsalted butter, at room temperature

Continued on page 118 »

» *Continued from page 116*

4 **BAKE THE CAKE**

Pour half the batter into the prepared Bundt pan. Set aside ½ cup of the toasted coconut for decorating the finished cake. Sprinkle the remaining 1 cup coconut evenly on top of the batter. Pour the remaining batter on top of the coconut. Bake the cake until it just starts to become light golden brown and a toothpick inserted near the center comes out clean, 35–40 minutes. Let cool in the pan on a wire rack for at least 20 minutes, then turn out onto the rack and let cool completely.

5 **MAKE THE GLAZE**

When the cake has cooled completely, make the glaze. In a small bowl, stir together the powdered sugar, 3 tablespoons of the coconut milk, the vanilla, and salt until smooth. Add more coconut milk, 1 teaspoon at a time, if needed. The glaze should be slightly thick but still pourable. Place the cake on the wire rack on a rimmed baking sheet. Using a spoon, slowly drizzle the glaze over the top of the cake, allowing it to run down the inside and outside of the ring. While the glaze is still wet, sprinkle the reserved toasted coconut over the center ring of the cake. Let set until the glaze is dry, about 15 minutes, before serving.

FOR THE GLAZE

½ cup powdered sugar

Reserved ¼ cup full-fat coconut milk

¼ teaspoon pure vanilla or coconut extract

Pinch of salt

CHOCOLATE CHIA PUDDING

Chia seeds are rich in omega-3 fatty acids, fiber, and protein. They have no flavor of their own, but when they are mixed into liquid, they thicken it naturally. Here they transform just a handful of ingredients—almond milk, cocoa powder, coconut sugar, and vanilla—into a delicious vegan dessert or snack that requires no cooking.

1 MAKE THE PUDDING BASE

In a jar that holds at least 2 cups liquid and has a tight-fitting lid, combine the cocoa powder and coconut sugar. Add ¼ cup of the almond milk, cover, and shake until combined. Add the remaining 1¼ cups almond milk and the vanilla, cover tightly, and shake to combine thoroughly with the chocolate mixture.

2 ADD THE CHIA SEEDS

Uncover the jar and add the chia seeds. Using a whisk or spoon, mix constantly until the chia seeds are evenly distributed and stay suspended in the liquid, about 5 minutes. Cover the jar and let it stand for 2 minutes. Shake the jar vigorously. Let stand for 2 minutes, then shake vigorously again. Repeat one more time.

3 CHILL & SERVE

Refrigerate the pudding in the jar until well chilled, at least 3 hours or up to overnight. Divide the pudding evenly among 3 small dessert bowls. Garnish with the raspberries and serve right away. This pudding is best served within 24 hours of being made.

» CHIA SEEDS come in black and in white. The difference is only aesthetic; nutritionally, they are identical.

2 tablespoons unsweetened natural cocoa powder

3 tablespoons coconut sugar

1½ cups unsweetened almond milk

1 teaspoon pure vanilla extract

5 tablespoons chia seeds

½ cup fresh raspberries

PEANUT BUTTER SANDWICH COOKIES

Oat flour and buckwheat flour take the place of all-purpose flour in these gluten-free treats. Don't include the filling, if you like, for a simpler and lighter option.

1 MAKE THE DOUGH

In a medium bowl, mix the oat and buckwheat flours, baking powder, baking soda, and salt. In a large bowl, using an electric mixer, beat the butter and granulated and brown sugars on medium-high speed until light and fluffy, about 3 minutes. Add the eggs, one at a time, beating well after each addition. Beat in the vanilla and peanut butter. Stop the mixer and scrape down the sides of the bowl with a rubber spatula. On low speed, add the flour mixture and beat just until combined. Cover the bowl and refrigerate until the dough is firm enough to scoop, about 2 hours.

2 BAKE THE COOKIES

Preheat the oven to 350°F. Line 2 rimmed baking sheets with parchment paper. Using a tablespoon, scoop balls of dough onto the prepared baking sheets, spacing the balls about 2 inches apart. Bake until the edges are golden brown, 8–10 minutes. Let the cookies cool on the pans on wire racks for 5 minutes, then transfer the cookies to the racks and let cool completely.

3 MAKE THE FILLING

In a bowl, using the electric mixer, beat together the peanut butter and butter on medium speed until combined, about 1 minute. Add the confectioners' sugar and beat until combined, about 1 minute. Add the milk and beat until smooth, about 30 seconds.

4 FILL THE COOKIES

Turn half of the cooled cookies flat side up on a work surface. Using a spoon, spread a heaping teaspoon of the filling onto each cookie. Top with the remaining cookies, flat side down. Store in an airtight container in the refrigerator for up to 4 days.

FOR THE COOKIES

1 cup oat flour

⅓ cup buckwheat flour

½ teaspoon baking powder

½ teaspoon baking soda

½ teaspoon salt

½ cup unsalted butter, at room temperature

½ cup granulated sugar

½ cup firmly packed light brown sugar

2 large eggs

1 teaspoon pure vanilla extract

1 cup creamy peanut butter

FOR THE FILLING

½ cup creamy peanut butter, at room temperature

3 tablespoons unsalted butter, at room temperature

½ cup confectioners' sugar

2 tablespoons whole milk

» OAT FLOUR is hearty yet light and buckwheat flour is dark and has a nutty flavor, making these two gluten-free options the perfect flavor partners for these delicious cookies.

BASIC RECIPES

BASIL PESTO

MAKES ABOUT 1 CUP

1 or 2 cloves garlic
¼ cup pine nuts
2 cups packed fresh basil leaves
½ cup extra-virgin olive oil
½ cup freshly grated Parmesan cheese
Salt and freshly ground pepper

With a food processor running, drop the garlic through the feed tube and process until minced. Turn off the processor, add the pine nuts, and pulse a few times to chop. Add the basil and pulse a few times to chop coarsely. Then, with the processor running, add the oil through the feed tube in a slow, steady stream and process until a smooth, moderately thick paste forms, stopping to scrape down the bowl with a rubber spatula as needed. Transfer to a bowl and stir in the Parmesan cheese. Season to taste with salt and freshly ground pepper. Use at once, or transfer to an airtight container, top with a thin layer of oil, cover, and refrigerate for up to 1 week.

COOKED CHICKEN

MAKES 1–2 SERVINGS

1–2 boneless, skinless chicken breasts
¼–½ teaspoon salt
¼ teaspoon black peppercorns
1 clove garlic, smashed
4 fresh herb sprigs, such as thyme or parsley

Put the chicken in a single layer in a saucepan. Add water to cover by 1–2 inches. Add the salt, peppercorns, garlic, and herbs. Bring to a boil over medium-high heat, then immediately reduce the heat to low, cover, and simmer until the chicken is opaque throughout, 10–14 minutes. Transfer the chicken to a cutting board and let cool, then use as directed, or refrigerate in an airtight container for up to 3 days.

PICO DE GALLO

MAKES ABOUT 2½ CUPS

2 large, ripe tomatoes, halved, seeded, and diced
½ cup finely chopped yellow onion
3 tablespoons minced fresh cilantro
1 tablespoon fresh lime juice
½ jalapeño chile, seeded and minced, or more to taste
Salt

In a glass or ceramic bowl, combine the tomatoes, onion, cilantro, lime juice, and chile and stir to mix well. Season to taste with salt. Cover and let stand at room temperature for at least 30 minutes or up to 3 hours before serving. Any leftover salsa can be stored in an airtight container in the refrigerator for up to 3 days.

STEAMED QUINOA

MAKES ABOUT 3 CUPS

1 cup quinoa, rinsed

2 cups water or reduced-sodium chicken broth

½ teaspoon salt

In a saucepan, bring the quinoa, water, and salt to a boil over high heat. Reduce the heat to low, give the quinoa a stir, cover, and cook, without lifting the lid, until the liquid is absorbed and the quinoa is tender, about 15 minutes. Remove from the heat and let stand, covered, for 5 minutes. Uncover, fluff with a fork, and serve.

STEAMED BROWN RICE

MAKES ABOUT 3 CUPS

1 cup short-grain brown rice

2 cups water

In a saucepan, combine the rice, water, and salt and bring to a boil over high heat. Reduce the heat to low, give the rice a stir, then cover and cook, without lifting the lid, until the liquid is absorbed and the rice is tender, 45–50 minutes. Remove from the heat and let stand, covered, for 10 minutes. Uncover, fluff with a fork, and serve.

STEAMED WHITE RICE

MAKES ABOUT 3 CUPS

1 cup long-grain white rice, such as jasmine or basmati

1½ cups water

In a saucepan, combine the rice and water. Bring to a boil over high heat. Reduce the heat to low, give the rice a stir, then cover and cook, without lifting the lid, until the liquid is absorbed and the rice is tender, about 20 minutes. Remove from the heat and let stand, covered, for 10 minutes. Uncover, fluff with a fork, and serve.

TZATZIKI

MAKES ABOUT 1¾ CUPS

1 container (7 oz/220 g) plain Greek-style yogurt

1 cup grated or finely diced English cucumber

1 garlic clove, minced

1 teaspoon minced fresh mint

1 teaspoon minced fresh dill

In a small bowl, mix together the yogurt, cucumber, garlic, mint, and dill. Set aside at room temperature for up to 1 hour, or cover and refrigerate for up to 3 days. Bring to room temperature before serving.

VIETNAMESE DIPPING SAUCE

MAKES ABOUT ¾ CUP

3 tablespoons fresh lime juice

2 tablespoons sugar

½ cup water

2½ tablespoons Asian fish sauce

1 fresh Thai chile, thinly sliced (optional)

In a small bowl, stir together the lime juice and sugar until the sugar dissolves. Add the water, fish sauce, and Thai chile (if using), and stir well.

INDEX

THE HEALTHY JUNIOR CHEF COOKBOOK

Conceived and produced by Weldon Owen International
in collaboration with Williams Sonoma, Inc.
3250 Van Ness Avenue, San Francisco, CA 94109

A WELDON OWEN PRODUCTION

1150 Brickyard Cove Road
Richmond, CA 94801
www.weldonowen.com

Copyright ©2020 Weldon Owen
and Williams Sonoma, Inc.
All rights reserved, including the right of reproduction
in whole or in part in any form.

Printed in China
10 9 8 7 6 5 4 3 2

Library of Congress
Cataloging-in-Publication data is available.

ISBN: 978-1-68188-518-6

WELDON OWEN INTERNATIONAL

CEO Raoul Goff
President Kate Jerome
Publisher Roger Shaw
Associate Publisher Amy Marr
Senior Editor Lisa Atwood
Assistant Editor Jourdan Plautz

Creative Director Chrissy Kwasnik
Art Director & Illustrator Marisa Kwek
Designer Megan Sinead Harris

Managing Editor Tarji Rodriguez
Production Manager Binh Au
Imaging Manager Don Hill

Photographer Erin Scott
Food Stylist Lillian Kang
Prop Stylist Claire Mack

Weldon Owen is a division of Insight Editions

ACKNOWLEDGMENTS

Weldon Owen wishes to thank the following people for their
generous support in producing this book: Lesley Bruynestyn, Bronwyn Lane,
Veronica Laramie, Elizabeth Parson, Sharon Silva, and Nick Wolf.